Language Handbook Worksheets

ELEMENTS OF

Literature

FIFTH COURSE

*Literature of the United States
with Literature of the Americas*

ADDITIONAL PRACTICE IN GRAMMAR, USAGE, AND MECHANICS

Correlated to Rules in the Language Handbook
in the Pupil's Edition, pages 1220–1257

HOLT, RINEHART AND WINSTON
Harcourt Brace & Company

Austin • New York • Orlando • Atlanta • San Francisco • Boston • Dallas • Toronto • London

Staff Credits

Associate Director: Mescal Evler

Manager of Editorial Operations: Robert R. Hoyt

Managing Editor: Bill Wahlgren

Project Editor: Katie Vignery

Component Editors: Marcia Kelley, Karen H. Kolar, James Hynes

Editorial Staff: *Associate Editors,* Kathryn Rogers, Christopher LeCluyse; *Assistant Managing Editor,* Mandy Beard; *Copyediting Supervisor,* Michael Neibergall; *Senior Copyeditor,* Mary Malone; *Copyeditors,* Joel Bourgeois, Jeffrey T. Holt, Suzi A. Hunn, Jane Kominek, Désirée Reid; *Editorial Coordinators,* Marie H. Price, Robert Littlefield, Mark Holland, Jill Chertudi, Tracy DeMont, Marcus Johnson; *Support Staff,* Pat Stover, Matthew Villalobos; *Word Processors,* Ruth Hooker, Margaret Sanchez, Kelly Keeley, Elizabeth Butler

Permissions: Tamara A. Blanken, Ann B. Farrar

Design: *Art Director, Book Design,* Richard Metzger; *Design Manager, Book & Media Design,* Joe Melomo

Prepress Production: Beth Prevelige, Simira Davis

Manufacturing Coordinator: Michael Roche

Printed in the United States of America

ISBN 0-03-052407-5

7 8 9 10 022 04 03 02 01

LANGUAGE HANDBOOK 1
THE PARTS OF SPEECH

LANGUAGE HANDBOOK 2
AGREEMENT

LANGUAGE HANDBOOK 3
USING VERBS

LANGUAGE HANDBOOK 4
USING PRONOUNS

LANGUAGE HANDBOOK 5
USING MODIFIERS

LANGUAGE HANDBOOK 6
PHRASES

LANGUAGE HANDBOOK 7
CLAUSES

LANGUAGE HANDBOOK 8
SENTENCE STRUCTURE

LANGUAGE HANDBOOK 9
SENTENCE STYLE

LANGUAGE HANDBOOK 10
SENTENCE COMBINING

LANGUAGE HANDBOOK 11
CAPITALIZATION

LANGUAGE HANDBOOK 12
PUNCTUATION

LANGUAGE HANDBOOK 13
PUNCTUATION

LANGUAGE HANDBOOK 14
SPELLING

LANGUAGE HANDBOOK 15
GLOSSARY OF USAGE

This booklet, *Language Handbook Worksheets*, contains practice and reinforcement copying masters that cover the material presented in the Language Handbook section of *Elements of Literature, Fifth Course*. The rules cited in the head of each worksheet correspond directly to the grammar, usage, and mechanics rules and instruction covered in the Language Handbook. Tests at the end of each section can be used either for assessment or for end-of-section reviews.

A separate *Answer Key* for the *Language Handbook Worksheets* provides answers or suggested responses to all items in this booklet.

For additional practice, instruction, and reinforcement in grammar, usage, and mechanics, refer to the following *Elements of Literature* ancillary:

- *Grammar and Language Link* These worksheets provide reinforcement, practice, and extension of the grammar and language skills presented in the Grammar Link and Language Link features in *Elements of Literature, Fifth Course*. Integrating language study with literature, worksheet examples and activities generally refer to the content of the selections.

LANGUAGE
HANDBOOK **1** **THE PARTS OF SPEECH**

WORKSHEET 1 | Identifying Nouns, Pronouns, and Adjectives

EXERCISE A   In the following sentences, underline each noun once and underline each pronoun twice.

> **EXAMPLE   1.** That is not the only reason Countee Cullen wrote poems.

1. Anyone can see the complex emotions in that painting.

2. Follow the signs to Gators Galore!

3. Whom are you offering to take besides me?

4. Mrs. Burgess, we read *The Life and Times of Frederick Douglass* at the end of last year.

5. Well, my car did not have a flat tire before this morning.

6. Three tall spires decorated the towers of the castle.

7. Steam engines, which once were the hope of car manufacturers, have never proved practical.

8. Did you make these yourself?

9. How many Americans have been awarded the Purple Heart?

10. After the competition, the crew threw a party for themselves and their friends from Port-au-Prince.

EXERCISE B   Underline each adjective in the following sentences. Do not underline the articles *a, an,* and *the.*

> **EXAMPLE   1.** Do you want another piece of whole-wheat toast?

1. For many centuries, the Chinese carefully guarded the secret of making silk cloth.

2. Rows of delicately carved figures decorated the Japanese vase.

3. In one short summer, he had grown taller, stronger, and more confident.

4. Please deliver these envelopes to the secretary in the main office.

5. Was this hammer the only one in the toolbox?

EXERCISE C   On the line provided, identify the italicized word in each of the following sentences. Write *N* for noun, *PRON* for pronoun, or *ADJ* for adjective.

> **EXAMPLE** ____N____ **1.** Is she really a *Kenyan*?

_____ **1.** Why does Swiss *cheese* have holes in it?

_____ **2.** A dozen *well-groomed* animals waited patiently outside the arena.

_____ **3.** Will *that* one be enough?

_____ **4.** The *Swiss* are known for their accurate chronometers.

_____ **5.** Those boots are *his.*

LANGUAGE HANDBOOK **1** **THE PARTS OF SPEECH**

WORKSHEET 2 | Identifying Verbs, Adverbs, Prepositions, Conjunctions, and Interjections

EXERCISE A For each of the following sentences, underline every word or word group that matches the part of speech indicated in parentheses.

> **EXAMPLE 1.** Quite <u>wisely</u>, African nations are <u>now</u> trying to protect their elephant populations. (*adverb*)

1. The precious crops of Africa's farmers, however, also deserve protection from the destruction that elephants can quickly wreak. (*preposition*)

2. Fortunately, his file had been saved recently, so he did not lose much of his essay. (*adverb*)

3. Gold, silver, and platinum are expensive, but they do not rust or corrode easily. (*conjunction*)

4. Merrily, the children had been chasing the dog as it tore through the house and dashed out the door. (*verb*)

5. That sunset didn't last long, but, oh, what a sight it was! (*interjection*)

6. Mix the first four ingredients and stir well; then, fold in the egg whites. (*verb*)

7. Neither Kyle nor Eva had a flashlight, so they couldn't explore the cave any farther. (*conjunction*)

8. The test was so easy that they finished early and did not stay for the whole period. (*adverb*)

9. Wow, you certainly dance well. (*interjection*)

10. In addition to the usual farm animals, a macaw was perched on the barn rafters and an emu was strolling in the paddock. (*preposition*)

EXERCISE B Identify the part of speech of each italicized word or word group in the following sentences. On the lines provided, write *V* for verb, *ADV* for adverb, *PREP* for preposition, *CONJ* for conjunction, or *INTER* for interjection.

> **EXAMPLE** ____*V*____ **1.** This machine *should have been oiled* long ago.

_____ 1. *Here* are the quarterly reports for your signature.

_____ 2. *Is* that the only way to arrive at a solution?

_____ 3. Everyone has been accounted for *but* Vera.

_____ 4. Has every element on the periodic table been fully studied *yet*?

_____ 5. Hummingbirds like red flowers, *yet* other birds seem to avoid them.

_____ 6. Do *not* bend, staple, or mutilate.

_____ 7. *Group* like items together.

_____ 8. The game was canceled *because of* rain.

_____ 9. *Yikes*! These plates are hot!

_____ 10. Ann is absent today *because* she is ill.

LANGUAGE HANDBOOK 1 THE PARTS OF SPEECH

WORKSHEET 3 | Test

EXERCISE A For each of the following sentences, underline each word or word group that matches the part of speech indicated in italics. Do not underline articles (*a*, *an*, or *the*) in the adjective items.

EXAMPLE *pronoun* **1.** "Take <u>me</u>, too," the toddler begged <u>her</u>.

noun **1.** Italian, Spanish, and Portuguese are all Romance languages.

pronoun **2.** This is just the product that everyone needs!

verb **3.** Should she have been keeping all those newspapers in the attic?

conjunction **4.** Either it will happen or it won't.

adverb **5.** Do not be so rude!

preposition **6.** Dozens of balloons filled with helium bobbed in the wind as he walked around.

pronoun **7.** Whom would you recommend to replace her?

verb **8.** Either oil or latex paint may be used, but do not use latex paint over oil paint.

adjective **9.** Fruits and vegetables are essential to a healthy body.

adverb **10.** Unfortunately, cobras sometimes menace the people of India.

preposition **11.** Dancers in elaborate costumes paraded through the streets on Mardi Gras evening.

adjective **12.** Use a decimal format for the third column of the spreadsheet.

noun **13.** The firm of Hartfield, Smith, and Finn, Incorporated, handles all our financial accounts.

conjunction **14.** What you and I need is a soft yet durable cloth for our sleeping bags.

preposition **15.** According to popular folklore, a wish on a star will come true.

verb **16.** Do you now know or have you ever known the defendant?

adjective **17.** A few days after the freeze, tiny, hard, green oranges covered the ground.

pronoun **18.** Both of us love the parade, which occurs every Chinese New Year.

adverb **19.** "Let me in immediately!" the cold, wet cat would have liked to say.

noun **20.** The strange code was actually instructions for an intricate pattern of stitches.

adjective **21.** With a mighty leap, she cleared the last hurdle.

verb **22.** The last time I saw you, you were taking Spanish classes.

conjunction **23.** Although it is small, an arrow from a wooden crossbow can be quite sharp and can pierce chain mail.

noun **24.** The sweet, heady scent of the English roses drifted onto the open patio.

pronoun **25.** Do you still want to build the doghouse by yourself?

Continued ☞

LANGUAGE HANDBOOK **1** **WORKSHEET 3** (continued)

EXERCISE B For each of the following sentences, identify the part of speech of the italicized word or word group. On the line provided, write *N* for noun, *PRON* for pronoun, *ADJ* for adjective, *V* for verb, *ADV* for adverb, *CONJ* for conjunction, *PREP* for preposition, or *INTER* for interjection.

EXAMPLE ___ADV___ **1.** Do tigers attack *only* from behind?

_____ **1.** Aren't you finished with the computer *yet*?

_____ **2.** *Who* was Billy Budd?

_____ **3.** Victorians were known for their *straight-laced* attitudes.

_____ **4.** Sailors on ships often sang *while* they were working.

_____ **5.** Recent excavations in China *unearthed* dinosaur fossils.

_____ **6.** The newly hatched baby quail followed him *everywhere*.

_____ **7.** New ideas and old ones clashed *throughout* the revolution.

_____ **8.** Your *sister-in-law* is one of the best coaches around.

_____ **9.** In the moonlight, the Japanese hills *appeared* almost mystical.

_____ **10.** Wow! Is that bike *yours*!

_____ **11.** Isn't that story *by* Isaac Bashevis Singer?

_____ **12.** What is the *Congressional Medal of Honor*?

_____ **13.** Yes, I *most* certainly will remember what you said.

_____ **14.** Are you going to wear *that* to the party?

_____ **15.** *Be* happy.

_____ **16.** *Bob Dylan* continues to be one of America's most influential songwriters.

_____ **17.** The Romantic poets were, *well*, romantic.

_____ **18.** Does this engine have *four* or six cylinders?

_____ **19.** *Few* of the rafters had ever seen rapids like these.

_____ **20.** A reliable system of dikes, ditches, *and* water wheels keeps the fields irrigated.

_____ **21.** Tallies showed the *electoral* vote was in our favor.

_____ **22.** The runner is sliding, and, *hooray,* he's safe at first.

_____ **23.** I plan to wear *either* the gray pants *or* the black ones.

_____ **24.** *In spite of* recent rains, creeks and streams were scarcely flowing.

_____ **25.** Will we still have the chemistry test *tomorrow*?

LANGUAGE HANDBOOK 2 AGREEMENT

WORKSHEET 1 | Making Subject and Verb Agree (Rules 2 a–c, i)

EXERCISE Wherever a phrase follows the subject, draw a line through it so that it won't mislead you. Then, underline the verb or helping verb that agrees in number with the subject. *Note:* Since some indefinite pronouns may be singular or plural, you may need to refer to the phrase after the subject to determine the number.

> EXAMPLES 1. One ~~of the sleeves~~ (look, <u>looks</u>) too short.
>
> 2. The biggest bargain (<u>is</u>, are) the raincoats.

1. A common name for the Dakota people (*is, are*) Sioux.

2. A few words of encouragement (*helps, help*) one to succeed.

3. The motto of *The New York Times* (*is, are*) "All the News That's Fit to Print."

4. One of the two theaters (*has, have*) been closed.

5. The new tires (*was, were*) my biggest expense.

6. My biggest expense (*was, were*) the new tires.

7. One of the wheels (*doesn't, don't*) turn freely.

8. The price of diamonds (*depends, depend*) on their size and quality.

9. Paints (*is, are*) Yoshi's only extravagance.

10. One cause of traffic congestion (*is, are*) poor planning.

11. Mr. Babinski, assisted by his two sons, (*operates, operate*) a garage.

12. The Organization of American States (*includes, include*) over thirty Latin American nations.

13. One of the members (*supplies, supply*) refreshments for each meeting.

14. The concert proceeds, collected at the door, (*goes, go*) to charity.

15. Their greatest concern (*is, are*) their children.

16. The results of the election (*was, were*) a tribute to Shirley Chisholm.

17. The humanitarian efforts of Eleanor Roosevelt (*was, were*) well-known during her lifetime.

18. Estella's main annoyance at this campsite (*is, are*) the mosquitoes.

19. Some of the letters (*has, have*) fallen off the sign.

20. Not a single original Shakespeare manuscript, of either his plays or his sonnets, (*exists, exist*) today.

21. Several of her books (*is, are*) available in paperback.

22. None of her books (*is, are*) available in paperback.

23. The woman playing checkers in the park (*find, finds*) it difficult to concentrate.

24. Not all of the students (*understand, understands*) the assignment.

25. The goal of our efforts (*justify, justifies*) the means.

LANGUAGE HANDBOOK **2** AGREEMENT

WORKSHEET 2 | **Making Subject and Verb Agree (Rules 2 a–d)**

EXERCISE Underline the subject in each of the following sentences. Then, underline the verb form in parentheses that agrees with the subject in number.

> **EXAMPLES** 1. <u>Neither</u> of my brothers (*have*, <u>*has*</u>) ever had the mumps.
>
> 2. <u>Each</u> of these problems (<u>*is*</u>, *are*) difficult.

1. Mr. King and Ms. Jackson (*cater*, *caters*) parties and weddings.
2. Mr. King, along with Ms. Jackson, (*cater*, *caters*) parties and weddings.
3. A prize or a certificate (*are*, *is*) given to each winner.
4. Every one of these words (*comes*, *come*) from Latin or Greek.
5. (*Do*, *Does*) every one of these rooms need to be painted?
6. The design of the table and chairs (*have*, *has*) been improved.
7. Each of these questions (*is*, *are*) answered in the chapter.
8. The students or the teacher (*corrects*, *correct*) the daily exercises.
9. The price of a new engine and its installation (*were*, *was*) too expensive.
10. Neither of these dresses (*is*, *are)* easy to make.
11. A friendly note or a telephone call (*don't*, *doesn't*) take much time.
12. The shortage of goods and the abundance of money (*make*, *makes*) prices skyrocket.
13. These kinds of shoes (*are*, *is*) hard on feet.
14. Either of these streets (*runs*, *run*) to the river.
15. Every pupil's height and weight (*is*, *are*) recorded each year.
16. Every one of the menorah candles (*is*, *are*) lit on the last day of Hanukkah.
17. Neither the music nor the words (*seem*, *seems*) very original.
18. Neither the words nor the music (*seem*, *seems*) very original.
19. The morale of Helen and her family (*was*, *were*) very high.
20. Kindness, intelligence, or strength (*arouses*, *arouse*) admiration.
21. Nobody among my friends (*says*, *say*) anything bad about this movie.
22. That kind of music (*soothe*, *soothes*) its listeners.
23. Either Carole or Sandy (*is*, *are*) playing goalie tonight.
24. Neither the bandleader nor the musicians (*know*, *knows*) that song.
25. (*Does*, *Do*) anyone hear the rumbling of thunder?

LANGUAGE
HANDBOOK **2** AGREEMENT

WORSHEET 3 | **Some Subject-Verb Agreement Problems (Rules 2 c–h)**

EXERCISE Underline the subject in each of the following sentences. Then, underline the word or words in parentheses that agree with the subject in number.

> EXAMPLE **1.** Where (*is*, _are_) the <u>Orkney Islands</u> located?

1. Approximately one sixth of a person's daily energy requirement (*is, are*) provided by a pint of milk.

2. (*Here's, Here are*) the spoons for the gazpacho.

3. *Blue Highways*, which is full of fascinating anecdotes, (*chronicle, chronicles*) the travels of William Least Heat-Moon.

4. There (*has, have*) been too many traffic accidents on this road.

5. Ever since its first screening, *Raiders of the Lost Ark* (*has, have*) captivated audiences.

6. (*There's, There are*) a row of poplar trees between the two farms.

7. (*Where's, Where are*) the keys to the luggage?

8. In which drawer (*is, are*) the stamps?

9. "Still Just Writing" (*describe, describes*) the somewhat humorous plight of writer Anne Tyler.

10. Why (*doesn't, don't*) someone write to author Jamaica Kincaid?

11. How much (*is, are*) those boxes of stationery?

12. The entire faculty (*was, were*) seated in the first four rows at our graduation.

13. The audience (*was, were*) rattling their programs.

14. The team (*has, have*) yet to win its first game.

15. The class (*was, were*) checking their test papers.

16. The first ten minutes of the film (*is, are*) very boring.

17. Five dollars (*seems, seem*) a fair price for this dreidel.

18. Only two lemons (*is, are*) needed for this recipe.

19. Two or more inches of mulch (*protects, protect*) many outdoor plants throughout the winter.

20. Over eight thousand thin sheets of gold (*was, were*) used to cover the spire of the Shwe Dagon Pagoda in Myanmar.

21. There (*was, were*) several vacant seats in the last row.

22. (*Is, Are*) there no bananas left for us?

23. Alfred Hitchcock's *The Birds* (*is, are*) coming to our local revival theater.

24. Twenty-five out of thirty students in the class (*is, are*) going to see the film.

25. Here (*come, comes*) the movers with our stove.

NAME _____ CLASS _____ DATE _____

LANGUAGE HANDBOOK **2** AGREEMENT

WORKSHEET 4 | Making Pronouns and Antecedents Agree
(Rules 2 j, k)

EXERCISE A   In the following sentences, draw a line through any pronoun that does not agree in gender or number with its antecedent. Then, write the correct form of the pronoun on the line provided. In several sentences, you will also need to change the verb.

EXAMPLES _he or she gets_ 1. A person tries harder if ~~they get~~ a little encouragement.

_____he_____ 2. Before a boy is accepted for the team, ~~they~~ must pass a physical test.

_____ 1. Whenever some of our class are late, Ms. Perez makes him or her write essays on promptness.

_____ 2. A cat will often attach itself to any family that feeds them.

_____ 3. Whether somebody was born in this country or is a naturalized citizen, they have an equal voice in the government.

_____ 4. Some careless camper had failed to put out their fire.

_____ 5. Why don't you girls get yourself something to read?

_____ 6. Whenever someone enters the lobby, a statue of Bolívar is the first thing they see.

_____ 7. If an egg floats in a pan of cold water, they are not fresh.

_____ 8. An applicant often can't get good jobs if they aren't college-educated.

_____ 9. When he or she celebrates the birthday of Ganesh, many Hindus parade his statue through the streets.

_____ 10. Most things are less expensive when you buy it in large quantities.

EXERCISE B   On the lines provided in each of the following sentences, write a pronoun or pair of pronouns that agrees in number and gender with its antecedent. Underline the antecedent in each sentence.

EXAMPLE **1.** Any interested <u>student</u> may submit _his or her_ portfolio to the yearbook editor.

1. Once a car starts across the bridge, _____ can't turn back.

2. Some readers like this mystery story because it keeps _____ guessing.

3. You can't make a child independent by doing everything for _____.

4. If a person parks in the municipal lot without paying, the police tow _____ car away.

5. After a customer has worn a dress, _____ cannot return it.

6. Tom shouldn't talk about _____ all the time. (*reflexive*)

7. Graduates should choose colleges that are outstanding in the fields that interest _____.

8. Whenever anyone gives directions, _____ should make _____ very clear.

9. If a person is a beginner at tennis, _____ can't expect to win often.

10. After reading one of Gwendolyn Brooks's poems, you can never forget _____.

8 *Language Handbook Worksheets*   *Elements of Literature*

Copyright © by Holt, Rinehart and Winston. All rights reserved.

WORKSHEET 5 | **Making Pronouns and Antecedents Agree (Rules 2 j–m)**

EXERCISE A In each of the following sentences, underline the pronoun or pair of pronouns in parentheses that is appropriate for careful formal writing. Then, underline the antecedent of the pronoun you have chosen.

> EXAMPLE **1.** <u>Many</u> of the Australian Aborigines who speak Guwal speak a special language called Dyalnguy when speaking to (<u>*their*</u>, *his*) mothers-in-law.

1. Wow! Both of the runners finished simultaneously, so (*they, it*) will have to race again.

2. No one should be made to feel that (*he or she, they*) must like sashimi.

3. Each one of the girls built (*herself, themselves*) a work area.

4. All of our students expecting to graduate should be sure that (*his or her, their*) credits have been checked.

5. Don't offer a ride to anybody unless you know (*him or her, them*).

6. At that time, few among the anthropologists spoke the language of (*his or her, their*) hosts.

7. Most of our preparation showed (*its, their*) worth.

8. Several of the bucks had already lost (*his, their*) antlers.

9. Wisely, many in the audience had secured (*his or her, their*) seats early.

10. Several of the girls had read the book, so the film's ending didn't surprise (*her, them*).

EXERCISE B Underline the correct pronoun in parentheses in each of the following sentences.

> EXAMPLE **1.** Neither Micah nor Jerry thinks Speech and Drama II is the course for (<u>*him*</u>, *them*).

1. If you see Darnell and Vic, tell (*them, him*) about the meeting.

2. If you see Darnell or Vic, tell (*them, him*) about the meeting.

3. That restaurant's food and service are better than (*they, it*) used to be.

4. Does an oak or a maple shed (*its, their*) leaves earlier in the fall?

5. Shawn takes math and chemistry because she needs (*it, them*) for engineering.

6. If the jacket or the coat is too long, you can shorten (*it, them*).

7. Both Alice and Maria wondered if Maria had jumper cables with (*her, them*).

8. If you want a good meal or snack, you can get (*it, them*) at Bruno's.

9. My little sister Raquel grabbed our ball and bat and ran away with (*them, it*).

10. Food and clothing are more expensive than (*it, they*) used to be.

LANGUAGE HANDBOOK 2 AGREEMENT

| WORKSHEET 6 | **Making Pronouns and Antecedents Agree (Rules m–p)** |

EXERCISE A Underline the correct pronoun in parentheses in each of the following sentences.

> **EXAMPLE 1.** Neither David nor his brothers remembered to bring (*his*, *their*) books.

1. Will Mrs. Hann or your friends give you (*her*, *their*) support?

2. Neither Joy nor the children could contain (*her*, *their*) glee at seeing an elephant.

3. Either squirrels or an opossum has made (*their*, *its*) home in the big oak tree.

4. Why would either Judy or her sisters ignore (*her*, *their*) own self-interest?

5. Neither the defendant nor the accomplices would admit (*her*, *their*) guilt.

6. Either our adult dogs or the puppies chewed (*its*, *their*) blanket into pieces.

7. Callahan Supplies shipped lumber and hardware from (*its*, *their*) Burnet Road store.

8. Neither the maple tree nor our shrubs lost (*its*, *their*) leaves before the first snow.

9. Either snow or ice has taken (*its*, *their*) toll on the roads and traffic.

10. Neither Sharla nor her friends have bought (*her*, *their*) tickets for the band concert.

EXERCISE B On the lines provided, rewrite each of the following sentences to avoid ambiguous or awkward constructions. More than one answer is possible.

> **EXAMPLE 1.** Neither the council members nor the mayor was willing to put her views on record. *The council members were not willing to put their views on record, and neither was the mayor willing to put hers on record.*

1. I couldn't tell whether Steve or the other players made their move first. _____

_____

2. Either Russell or his brothers are going to the museum with their class. _____

_____

3. We were surprised that neither Ellen nor her sisters had eaten their breakfast. _____

_____

4. Neither the president nor his opponents will announce their legislative strategy in advance.

_____

_____

5. I found out that either Laura or her cousins got their chores done early. _____

_____

Continued ☞

Elements of Literature

EXERCISE C For each of the following sentences, underline the pronoun in parentheses that correctly completes the sentence.

EXAMPLE **1.** The crowd began stamping (*their*, *its*) feet.

1. *Great Expectations* should not be read in an abridged version; (*it*, *they*) can be truly appreciated only in full.

2. We watched in amazement as the swarm left (*their*, *its*) hive and soared upward.

3. Many people go to the Philippines this time of year; have you considered (*it*, *them*) for your vacation?

4. Any society must maintain traditions, or (*they*, *it*) will disintegrate and be lost to future generations.

5. Señor Montoya's herd was ready, but he had no one to drive (*them*, *it*) to market.

6. Has Clark Brothers Appliances made Sunlight Shopping Center (*their*, *its*) new location?

7. When smoke filled the theater, the audience quickly left (*its*, *their*) seats and hurried out the exits.

8. The graduating class threw (*its*, *their*) hats in the air.

9. "Happy Trails" not only became Roy Rogers's theme song, but (*they*, *it*) became the lullaby for a generation.

10. The band practiced (*its*, *their*) most popular numbers.

11. The hen watched her brood of chicks as (*it*, *they*) pecked at the feed.

12. At last, the council voted on the plans for (*its*, *their*) new meeting room.

13. How did the jury decide whether (*its*, *their*) verdict would be "guilty" or "innocent"?

14. Color a dozen of the eggs at a time, and set (*it*, *them*) here to dry.

15. Yesterday, we discussed "The Weary Blues" and (*its*, *their*) connection to jazz.

16. Forest Fitness offers its clientele (*its*, *their*) own personalized training routines.

17. Because of (*its*, *their*) poor organization, the posse had not yet caught the bandits.

18. We like the Cool Ices shops and hope to see more of (*it*, *them*) open in town.

19. Every summer, the youth of our city spend much of (*its*, *their*) time at the city park.

20. Since I read "God's Trombones," (*it's*, *they've*) become one of my favorite poems.

21. Do you know what wildlife makes (*its*, *their*) home in a burrow like that?

22. Please ask the staff to bring note-taking materials with (*it*, *them*) to our next meeting.

23. Today's Plants advertised that (*it*, *they*) would give away one seedling with any purchase.

24. At rehearsal, the choir practiced (*its*, *their*) parts before singing the school song.

25. The throng headed for the beach and took umbrellas and towels with (*it*, *them*).

LANGUAGE HANDBOOK **2** AGREEMENT

WORKSHEET 7 | Test (Rules 2 a–p)

EXERCISE A   If the italicized verb in each of the sentences does not agree in number with its subject, write the correct form of the verb on the line provided. If a sentence is already correct, write *C*.

EXAMPLE ___was___   **1.** The bald eagle, known for its flashing white feathers, *were* selected in 1782 as the emblem of the United States.

_____ **1.** The eagle's tremendous strength and courage *makes* it an impressive symbol for our country.

_____ **2.** Neither the bird nor its habits *is* known to most Americans.

_____ **3.** The eagle and its mate never *deserts* the original nest, which can weigh up to two tons.

_____ **4.** Thirty-five days *are* the usual incubation period, and each of the mates takes turns sitting on the eggs.

_____ **5.** Later, both the mother and the father *feeds* the young by tearing food into small pieces with their beaks.

_____ **6.** Fish and, occasionally, small mammals *are* its favorite diet.

_____ **7.** Pesticides and the draining of wetlands *is* the greatest threat to eagles' survival.

_____ **8.** Congress *have* passed legislation to protect this noble bird.

_____ **9.** The shooting of a bald eagle or the theft of its eggs *are* prohibited by law.

_____ **10.** Even possession of eagle feathers *are* illegal unless you are an American Indian.

EXERCISE B   Most of the following sentences contain verbs that do not agree with their subjects. Draw a line through any incorrect verb. Then, on the line provided, write the correct form of each verb. If a sentence is correct, write *C*.

EXAMPLE ___holds___   **1.** Sandra Cisneros' work, which sometimes blends Spanish and English, ~~hold~~ a unique place in American literature.

_____ **1.** The fear of overpopulating arable lands shape China's internal policies.

_____ **2.** Trees in this forest constitutes a major resource for the nearby communities.

_____ **3.** Broken tiles of every color have been embedded in the walkways of this park.

_____ **4.** Students who had not registered for classes was reporting to the auditorium.

_____ **5.** Vaccines that were developed during the last century is still saving many lives.

Continued ☞

LANGUAGE HANDBOOK 2 WORKSHEET 7 *(continued)*

EXERCISE C   Underline the verb in parentheses that correctly completes the sentence.

> **EXAMPLE 1.** In what part of the world (*is, are*) Ecuador located?

1. Where (*was, were*) everyone going?

2. Here (*is, are*) a few of the ways you can arrange a chart like this.

3. There (*was, were*) a great many issues raised at the meeting.

4. (*There's, There are*) no reason for all this fuss.

5. Hey, Robby! (*Here's, Here are*) those books you were looking for this morning.

EXERCISE D   Most of the following sentences contain verbs that do not agree with their subjects. Underline the incorrect verbs. Then, on the line provided, write the correct form of each verb. If a sentence is already correct, write *C*.

> **EXAMPLE** ___*is*___ **1.** *Midnight Wheels* are always checked out.

_____ **1.** Los Angeles, whose name means "the angels" in Spanish, are often referred to simply as LA.

_____ **2.** When was the United Nations formed?

_____ **3.** The Netherlands, as you may know, border the North Sea.

_____ **4.** I wonder how much van Gogh's painting *Sunflowers* are worth these days.

_____ **5.** Do "Fire and Ice" present any contrasts?

_____ **6.** Look at all the vacation activities that the Hawaiian Islands area have to offer!

_____ **7.** *Apples and Oranges* are the title of the painting my uncle sold last week.

_____ **8.** My new friend lives in Fordham Oaks, which are not far from the lake.

_____ **9.** The Aleutian Islands are a chain of islands that extend from the Alaska Peninsula.

_____ **10.** We presented our skit "Rings and Circles," which were applauded by the class.

EXERCISE E   Underline the verb in parentheses that correctly completes each of the following sentences.

> **EXAMPLE 1.** One of the main ingredients of success (*is, are*) long hours.

1. The only requirement for entrance (*is, are*) good grades.

2. (*Weren't, Wasn't*) the best part of the circus the clowns?

3. Good manners (*is, are*) your best introduction.

4. The way your parents lived (*is, are*) not necessarily the way you will live.

5. Difficult experiences (*has, have*) become one of Gary Soto's great sources of insight.

Continued ☞

EXERCISE F   Underline the pronoun in parentheses that correctly completes each of the following sentences.

> **EXAMPLE 1.** Neither Valentina nor her friend Maria had pictures of (*their*, *her*) Venezuelan home.

1. Our congregation prides (*themselves*, *itself*) on singing well and loudly.

2. Yellow and orange lend (*its*, *their*) warm hues to the cozy room.

3. Did any of the movie deliver what (*it*, *they*) promised?

4. Too often a crowd sweeps everyone along with (*it*, *them*).

5. The new Two Brothers is a restaurant; (*it*, *they*) will open next Friday.

6. How may Japan or Korea develop (*its*, *their*) economy in the next century?

7. All of these garments can be purchased from (*its*, *their*) designers.

8. Either Janie or the Stedmans will do (*her*, *their*) best to get the flowers to the church on time.

9. Several of the artworks in the museum clearly reflected (*its*, *their*) African heritage.

10. Everybody will rise from (*his or her*, *their*) chair when the national anthem is played.

11. Neither my aunt nor my cousins want (*her*, *their*) lunch.

12. The drama class will present the play *Raindrops and Icicles*, which has three acts in (*it*, *them*).

13. Both my brother and his employees enjoyed (*his*, *their*) day off from work.

14. The bull and bear stock markets have (*its*, *their*) own distinctive characteristics.

15. One of the most amazing facts about the lizard has to do with (*its*, *their*) tail.

16. Sandra studied for the test by (*herself*, *itself*) after she had studied with us.

17. Every voter in that precinct had plenty of time to cast (*his or her*, *their*) vote.

18. When do droplets of water change (*its*, *their*) form into ice crystals?

19. The hogs are waiting for this bucket of corn for (*its*, *their*) dinner.

20. Jeff stopped at Bringing You Flowers to see if (*he*, *they*) could buy yellow roses.

21. Each council member must file a statement of (*his or her*, *their*) campaign expenses.

22. Our graduating class should seat (*itself*, *themselves*) in the assigned rows.

23. Either Fred or Nathan will give (*his*, *their*) speech tomorrow.

24. Traffic lights on Main Street were not changing the way (*it*, *they*) usually did.

25. Pinto beans should be soaked and rinsed before (*it's*, *they're*) cooked.

| LANGUAGE HANDBOOK | **3** | USING VERBS |

| **WORKSHEET 1** | Using Regular and Irregular Verbs (Rules 3 a–c) |

EXERCISE   In the following sentences, underline the correct form of each italicized verb in parentheses.

> **EXAMPLE 1.** When Gwendolyn Brooks was fifteen, she (*began*, *begun*) mailing her poems to James Weldon Johnson, who (*wrote*, *written*) back to encourage her.

1. The boxes that Yusuf tried to take to India (*are*, *were*) too heavy to carry on the plane.

2. Florence Nightingale (*did*, *done*) as much as she could have (*did*, *done*).

3. As soon as I had (*ate*, *eaten*) the curry, I (*paid*, *had paid*) the check and left a tip.

4. Dad had (*swam*, *swum*) out to the boat to see if he could start the engine.

5. I (*drank*, *drunk*) the water after I had (*catch*, *caught*) my breath.

6. We have (*flew*, *flown*) to Monterrey, Mexico, and we have also (*drove*, *driven*) there.

7. We might (*have get*, *have gotten*) to the park by noon if we (*started*, *had started*) earlier.

8. The model that was (*chose*, *chosen*) was (*built*, *builded*) by Corita.

9. I (*have carried*, *carried*) in the lawn chairs before the wind could blow them over.

10. If Pang had not been wearing a life jacket, he might (*drown*, *have drowned*).

11. Our dog climbed out of the pool and (*shaked*, *shook*) water on everyone.

12. We had (*lended*, *lent*) several books to him, but he never brought them back.

13. Each child attacked the piñata with a stick until the figure (*broke*, *had broken*) open.

14. Lars Riedel of Germany (*throwed*, *threw*) the discus 227 feet, 8 inches at the 1996 Summer Olympics and (*sat*, *set*) a new Olympic record.

15. Li (*brung*, *brought*) over some posters he had (*drew*, *drawn*).

16. When I (*came*, *come*) into the living room, the movie had already (*began*, *begun*).

17. On Thanksgiving, I had (*gone*, *went*) to the homeless shelter and (*lent*, *lend*) a hand serving food.

18. She gave us the apples that had (*fell*, *fallen*) from the tree.

19. Thelma, would you see that the lettuce (*is torn*, *has been torn*) into small pieces and the tomatoes (*are sliced*, *had been sliced*) for a salad?

20. In Australian Aboriginal cultures, boomerangs (*will have been*, *have been*) used as tools, toys, weapons, musical instruments, and trading objects.

21. After I had (*finish*, *finished*) carving the turkey, I (*carry*, *carried*) the platter into the dining room.

22. The author Joseph Conrad (*had*, *will have*) been a professional seaman before he (*became*, *had become*) a writer.

23. If my father (*has*, *had*) his way, we will finish our Christmas shopping by Thanksgiving this year.

24. Next year, our school play (*will have been*, *will be*) *The Importance of Being Earnest*.

25. By the time the movie (*finished*, *finishes*), the audience (*will be*, *will have been*) sitting in the theater for three hours.

LANGUAGE HANDBOOK	**3**	USING VERBS

WORKSHEET 2 **Using Regular and Irregular Verbs (Rules 3 a–c)**

EXERCISE A Underline the correct form of each italicized verb in parentheses in the following sentences.

> **EXAMPLE 1.** Mohandas K. Gandhi, who (*lead, led*) India's independence
> movement, was also (*known, knew*) as Mahatma, meaning "great soul."

1. Botan and Yori had (*practice, practiced*) their judo techniques all morning, and they had (*became, become*) very hungry by lunchtime.

2. Farmers in the Rio Grande Valley of Texas worried when their citrus crops (*froze, frozen*).

3. We (*saw, seen*) a bus coming and (*ran, run*) to catch it.

4. Sonia (*has washed, washed*) her favorite sweater carefully in cold water and (*lay, laid*) it on a towel to dry so that the garment wouldn't (*shrink, have shrunk*).

5. Mr. Mastroangelo (*teaches, has taught*) band at Winola High School for fifteen years and (*has sent, sends*) many soloists to state competitions.

6. Someone (*stoled, stole*) my hat that I had (*wore, worn*) only once.

7. Bena wasn't sure she (*could keep, could have kept*) quiet much longer, as she had almost (*burst, bursted*) with excitement.

8. The tiny island of Montserrat in the Caribbean (*was shaking, was shaken*) by earthquakes many times before its volcano (*explodes, exploded*) on September 17, 1996.

9. A carillon is played by a musician who (*hits, hit*) keys and pedals attached to metal pieces that (*strike, struck*) bells.

10. The *Titanic* (*has taken, had taken*) on water for two and one-half hours before it (*had sunk, sank*).

11. I would have (*rode, ridden*) my bicycle if I had (*knew, known*) how far it was.

12. José (*found, finds*) that the ankle he sprained in soccer practice (*didn't hurt, hadn't hurt*) as much if he put ice on it.

13. After we (*spread, spreaded*) out the food that we (*buy, had bought*), we (*enjoyed, had enjoyed*) our picnic.

14. The song that they (*sang, sung*) at the awards banquet was (*wrote, written*) by Lusita.

15. Jesse and Clay (*swung, swang*) their partners a little too vigorously in the square dance, and the motion (*makes, made*) their partners dizzy.

16. The phone (*was ringing, had rung*) as I opened the door, but I (*let, had let*) the answering machine get the call.

17. The insurance for Tyrone's car (*costs, will cost*) less next year since he (*had, has had*) no accidents.

18. I would have (*spoke, spoken*) a little louder if I (*realize, had realized*) that the audience couldn't hear me.

Continued ☞

19. The blade of the power saw (*spinned, spun*) noisily as Cara (*cut, cuts*) into the hard mesquite wood.

20. If all of you (*have read, had read*) August Wilson's *The Piano Lesson* by tomorrow, we (*have held, will hold*) auditions to cast the play.

EXERCISE B   Write *past* before each past tense form that can be used without a helping verb. Write *have* before every past participle to show that it requires a helping verb. Then, for each past participle, write a short sentence using the past participle and its helping verb correctly.

EXAMPLES ___*past*___ **1.** did _____

___*have*___ **2.** written _*I have written my book report.*_____

_____ **1.** taken _____

_____ **2.** rode _____

_____ **3.** come _____

_____ **4.** done _____

_____ **5.** tore _____

_____ **6.** came _____

_____ **7.** begun _____

_____ **8.** went _____

_____ **9.** swam _____

_____ **10.** seen _____

_____ **11.** took _____

_____ **12.** spoken _____

_____ **13.** rang _____

_____ **14.** chose _____

_____ **15.** driven _____

_____ **16.** wore _____

_____ **17.** run _____

_____ **18.** stole _____

_____ **19.** worn _____

_____ **20.** gave _____

_____ **21.** flew _____

_____ **22.** began _____

_____ **23.** forgave _____

_____ **24.** frozen _____

_____ **25.** drank _____

LANGUAGE HANDBOOK **3** USING VERBS

Using *Lie/Lay, Sit/Set,* and *Rise/Raise* Correctly (Rules 3 a, b)

EXERCISE Underline the correct form of each italicized verb in parentheses in the following sentences.

> **EXAMPLE 1.** Just as we (*sat, set*) down, everyone else (*rose, raised*) to applaud the speaker.

1. (*Lie, Lay*) your work aside and (*lie, lay*) down for a short rest.

2. Why didn't Leon (*sit, set*) where the others (*sat, set*)?

3. Although prices (*rose, raised*), earnings didn't (*rise, raise*).

4. If you (*lie, lay*) down, I'll (*lie, lay*) a cold cloth on your head.

5. We (*sat, set*) the gift where Ms. Currie was going to (*sit, set*).

6. The roots of the tree have (*risen, raised*) the sidewalk.

7. Lin (*lay, laid*) awake, wondering where she had (*lain, laid*) her catcher's mitt.

8. My backpack was still (*sitting, setting*) where I had (*sat, set*) it.

9. Gasoline taxes have (*risen, rose*) greatly during recent years.

10. My note has (*lain, laid*) on Mr. Garza's desk since I (*laid, lay*) it there.

11. I (*sat, set*) my CD player on the table and (*sat, set*) down to listen.

12. When the curtain (*rose, raised*), a stagehand was still on the stage.

13. Your books will (*lie, lay*) there until you (*lie, lay*) them elsewhere.

14. Don't (*sit, set*) the eggs where someone might (*sit, set*) on them.

15. Armando (*rose, raised*) his hand and (*rose, raised*) to ask a question.

16. I found my keys (*lying, laying*) where I usually (*lie, lay*) them.

17. I (*sat, set*) my chair back to avoid the draft.

18. As the water flows into the lock, the ship gradually (*rises, raises*).

19. I (*lay, laid*) in bed longer than I should have after the alarm rang.

20. The audience had just (*risen, rose*) to sing the national anthem.

21. When Emilia (*rose, raised*) from her seat, she found the book on the table where she had (*lain, laid*) it.

22. Paul (*sat, set*) the food dish quietly on the floor, near where the cat (*lie, lay*).

23. When the teacher (*set, sat*) the speech before her, Francesca (*raised, rose*) to the occasion.

24. Mr. Yamamoto (*raises, rises*) the flower box off the porch where it has been (*lying, laying*) all night.

25. (*Lay, Lie*) the package on the table and (*sit, set*) down while I (*raise, rise*) the window.

LANGUAGE HANDBOOK **3** **USING VERBS**

WORKSHEET 4 Using Correct Verb Tenses (Rules 3 a, b)

EXERCISE A   In each of the following sentences, underline the verb tense in parentheses that expresses the time relationship more accurately.

> **EXAMPLE 1.** From the time we grew a potato plant in second grade, my brother and I (*have been, are*) interested in horticulture.

1. Ever since we moved to the city, we (*grew, have grown*) houseplants.

2. When we first began growing them, they often (*died, have died*).

3. One geranium (*lived, has lived*) for a few days and then suddenly died.

4. During the past month our plants (*flourished, have flourished*) remarkably.

5. They (*revived, have revived*) since we began giving them less water.

6. Before we read plant-care books, we (*watered, have watered*) the plants too much.

7. Ever since we bought a full-spectrum light unit, we (*got, have gotten*) truly amazing results.

8. Compost also (*contributed, has contributed*) to our plants' good health.

9. The flowering plants (*began, have begun*) to bloom during the past week or two.

10. The foliage plants (*sprouted, have sprouted*) many new leaves.

EXERCISE B   On the line provided, write the past participle of each italicized verb (the past form required after any form of the linking verb *have*).

> **EXAMPLE 1.** (*throw*) had ___thrown___

1. (*begin*) has _____
2. (*break*) has _____
3. (*drink*) has _____
4. (*drive*) had _____
5. (*choose*) has _____
6. (*eat*) had _____
7. (*sing*) will have _____
8. (*swim*) have _____
9. (*tear*) has _____
10. (*see*) had _____

11. (*shake*) had _____
12. (*use*) has _____
13. (*ask*) have _____
14. (*go*) had _____
15. (*drown*) will have _____
16. (*lend*) has _____
17. (*be*) has _____
18. (*catch*) has _____
19. (*try*) had _____
20. (*say*) have _____

WORKSHEET 5 | Using Correct Verb Tenses (Rules 3 a, b)

EXERCISE A   For each of the following sentences, underline the form of the verb in parentheses that shows the order in which the actions occurred.

> **EXAMPLES 1.** Eileen refused the job, and Earl (_took_, *had taken*) it.
>
> **2.** Earl took the job that Eileen (*refused*, _had refused_).

1. Rosa paid for the library book that she (*lost, had lost*).

2. Eli never mentioned the money he (*borrowed, had borrowed*) from me.

3. The Turners rented a boat at the resort and (*went, had gone*) fishing.

4. I recalled a story I (*heard, had heard*) many years ago.

5. Miriam suddenly realized that she (*read, had read*) the wrong chapter.

6. Ida thought that she (*reached, had reached*) her goal.

7. Ms. Cruz showed movies of every country she (*visited, had visited*).

8. Mildred saw the advertisement and (*applied, had applied*) for the job.

9. Some people feel that Lincoln's speech at Gettysburg (*was, had been*) a failure.

10. We knew all along that Awan (*took, had taken*) our picture.

EXERCISE B   In each of the following sentences, underline the verb in parentheses that is in the proper tense.

> **EXAMPLE 1.** In May we (*will live*, _will have lived_) in this house ten years.

1. By learning to read faster, you (*will save, will have saved*) much time.

2. After I pay for this book, I (*will spend, will have spent*) my last cent.

3. If Kareem (*had debated, would have debated*), we would have won.

4. By tomorrow, this car (*will travel, will have traveled*) 100,000 miles.

5. If you follow a schedule, you (*will do, will have done*) better work.

6. If you (*had tried, would have tried*) the mulligatawny soup, you would have liked it.

7. By the time you receive this card, I (*had, shall have had*) my room painted.

8. If we win this match, we (*shall win, shall have won*) six straight sets.

9. When I sell two more tickets, I (*shall sell, shall have sold*) my quota.

10. If I (*had known, would have known*) your address, I would have written you a letter.

| WORKSHEET 6 | ### Avoiding Unnecessary Shifts in Verb Tense (Rules 3 a–c) |

EXERCISE A   The following sentences are written mainly in the present tense. Underline each verb that is mistakenly in the past tense. Then, on the line provided, write the correct present tense of the verb. If a sentence is already correct, write *C*.

EXAMPLE _____*is*_____ **1.** Mathilde is a pretty French woman who <u>was</u> married to a poor but pleasant clerk in the government service.

_____ **1.** Because of his small income, Mathilde's husband was not able to give her the life of luxury and romance for which she yearns.

_____ **2.** One day he joyously brings home an invitation to a fancy ball.

_____ **3.** His wife, however, is not happy because she lacked suitable jewels for such an affair.

_____ **4.** She solved her problem by borrowing a diamond necklace from a friend in better circumstances.

_____ **5.** After making a great hit at the ball because of her beauty, she finds, when she arrived home, that the necklace was gone.

_____ **6.** By going deeply into debt, she and her husband bought another necklace to replace the one they lost.

_____ **7.** For ten years they live in attics and scrimp and struggle to pay off their debt.

_____ **8.** During that time, she lost her beauty and became so plain and worn that no one can recognize her for the beautiful girl she once was.

_____ **9.** Once Mathilde and her husband are finally out of debt, Mathilde decided to tell her friend how she lost the borrowed necklace and supplied a substitute.

_____ **10.** "Oh, no Mathilde!" her friend gasped with amazement. "Why, the necklace I lent you was only paste!"

EXERCISE B   In each of the following sentences, the first verb is in the past tense and the second verb is in the present tense. If the shift to present tense is correct because the second part of the statement is a general truth, write *C* on the line provided. If the tense incorrectly shifts from past to present, underline the incorrect verb form and write the correct form on the line provided.

EXAMPLE _____*based*_____ **1.** The French scientists who invented the metric system <u>base</u> their system on the circumference of the earth.

_____ **1.** In science class we learned that most countries use the metric system.

Continued ☞

_____ **2.** Mrs. Katz brought metric measuring tools to class and shows us how to use them.

_____ **3.** She told us that scientists measure length in meters and centimeters.

_____ **4.** We discovered that a meter consists of one hundred equal parts, called centimeters.

_____ **5.** We placed two rulers side by side and compare one inch to one centimeter.

_____ **6.** All of us agreed that one inch equals approximately two-and-a-half centimeters.

_____ **7.** One student asked how scientists measure long distances.

_____ **8.** "In kilometers," replied a student who moves here from Mexico.

_____ **9.** Dolores explained that a kilometer is equal to one thousand meters, or about six tenths of a mile.

_____ **10.** We calculated that the sun is about 150 million kilometers from earth.

EXERCISE C   In the following paragraph the verb tenses are not consistent. Decide whether the paragraph should be in present or past tense. Then, draw a line through each verb you wish to change, and write the correct form above it to make the tenses consistent.

EXAMPLE   [1] In August, our family goes on vacation to the coast; because I

lets

have received my license, Dad ~~let~~ me drive part of the way.

or

went

EXAMPLE   [1] In August, our family ~~goes~~ on vacation to the coast; because I

had

~~have~~ received my license, Dad let me drive part of the way.

[1] We seldom spend much time in our rooms if we could help it. [2] The seashore, where we can enjoy swimming or go snorkeling, beckoned. [3] My little sister likes to hunt for seashells early in the morning before anyone else was on the beach. [4] She had good luck finding sand dollars and a variety of whelks that she can add to her collection. [5] In the evenings we like to sit at the top of the dunes, where we watched the stars come out.

LANGUAGE HANDBOOK **3** USING VERBS

WORKSHEET 7 Using Active Voice and Passive Voice (Rules 3 d, e)

EXERCISE A On the lines provided, rewrite each of the following sentences, changing the italicized verbs from passive voice to active voice. To make this change, place the performer of the action before the verb as its subject. If the performer of the action is not mentioned, leave the sentence as it is and write *C* for correct.

> **EXAMPLE 1.** The Cathedral of Hagia Sophia *was admired* by everyone in our
> tour group. *Everyone in our tour group admired the Cathedral of*
> *Hagia Sophia.*

1. A delicious aroma *was sent* through the house by the baking lasagna. _____

_____

2. Praise for a job well done *is appreciated* by everyone. _____

_____

3. The da Vinci masterpiece *was hung* in the Louvre in Paris. _____

_____

4. I *am expected* home at midnight by my parents. _____

_____

5. Many errors *were committed* in the baseball game. _____

_____

EXERCISE B On the lines provided, rewrite the following sentences in the passive voice. Start your sentence with the *thing or things acted upon* and omit *the performer* of the action.

> **EXAMPLE 1.** Sharon made many typographical errors in the yearbook captions.
> *Many typographical errors were made in the yearbook captions.*

1. A person can reach Jakarta by ship or plane. _____

_____

2. Pepe left the water running in the bathtub. _____

_____

3. Someone broke a window while we were away. _____

_____

4. The mechanic replaced the car's shock absorbers. _____

_____

5. John guarantees a splendid time for all. _____

_____

LANGUAGE HANDBOOK 3 USING VERBS

WORKSHEET 8 Test (Rules 3 a–e)

EXERCISE A Underline the correct past form of each italicized verb in parentheses.

> **EXAMPLE 1.** Leon (*sang*, _sung_) a song that had been (*wrote*, _written_) by his grandfather.

1. I (*began, begun*) to wonder if I had (*saw, seen*) a ghost.

2. The police must have (*knew, known*) who (*stole, stolen*) the car.

3. I had (*did, done*) every problem that Mrs. Gómez had (*gave, given*) us.

4. Dad (*came, come*) to the kitchen to see what had (*fell, fallen*).

5. Paula (*gave, given*) me a snapshot that she had (*took, taken*) of Tomás.

6. After we had (*drove, driven*) ten miles, we (*saw, seen*) our mistake.

7. Carla had just (*went, gone*) to the bank and (*withdrew, withdrawn*) her money.

8. I had (*grew, grown*) tired of the poster and had (*threw, thrown*) it out.

9. Hale (*ran, run*) to the door to see who had (*rang, rung*) the bell.

10. If you had (*wore, worn*) your gloves, you would not have (*froze, frozen*) your fingers.

EXERCISE B Underline the correct form of each italicized verb in parentheses.

> **EXAMPLE 1.** I have many wonderful teachers, but Mr. Sato (_is_, *was*) my favorite.

1. Ever since I heard this story about Mr. Sato, it (*has amused, amused*) me very much.

2. In his entire teaching career, Mr. Sato never (*was, has been*) late to school—and by the end of this semester, he (*will have taught, will teach*) twenty years!

3. He never (*was, has been*) absent.

4. Through the years, he always (*hopes, has hoped*) to keep up his perfect record.

5. Two years ago, he thought he (*lost, had lost*) it.

6. One dark morning in February, he woke up and (*looked, looks*) at his clock, which (*had stopped, stopped*) at seven o'clock.

7. For the first time, he must (*forgot, have forgotten*) to set it.

8. He dressed in a rush, skipped breakfast, and (*runs, ran*) to the corner for a bus.

9. The streets were unusually deserted, and no buses (*come, came*) along.

10. He hailed a taxi after he (*had waited, waited*) several minutes.

11. He urged the driver to hurry, for he (*was, is*) late for school.

12. The driver (*gave, gives*) him a funny look and (*starts, started*) the meter.

13. "By the time I arrive," Mr. Sato thought anxiously, "Mrs. Osgood (*will start, will have started*) my first-hour class."

14. He tried all the doors after he (*had arrived, arrived*) at school.

15. They were all locked, and the building (*is, was*) dark.

Continued ☞

16. He then went around to the maintenance office, where he (*knocks, knocked*) on the door.

17. The custodian came to the door and (*asked, asks*), "What are you doing here at five o'clock in the morning?"

18. "I (*hadn't opened, haven't opened*) the school yet," he continued.

19. "I didn't plan to arrive quite so early," (*replies, replied*) the chagrined Mr. Sato.

20. "Next time I (*will check, have checked*) a second clock."

EXERCISE C   Each of the following sentences is missing an irregular verb. The present form of the verb is printed in italics before the sentence. On the line provided, write the form of this verb that will complete the sentence correctly.

> EXAMPLE   *write*   **1.** Many dramatic stories have been __written__ about the heroism of the huskies of the Far North, but no dog has done more to deserve a hero's reward than Balto.

know   **1.** The world might never have _____ of Balto if a severe diphtheria epidemic had not broken out in Nome, Alaska, in 1925.

catch   **2.** A large number of children had _____ the dreaded disease, and the town's small supply of antitoxin had run out.

go   **3.** A terrific blizzard was raging, and the temperature had _____ down to 80 degrees below zero.

fly   **4.** No one knew if the plane could have _____ through such weather.

come   **5.** It was here that Balto _____ into the story.

choose   **6.** Gunnar Kaasen volunteered his services, and his young lead dog, Balto, was _____ to be the leader of Kaasen's twelve-dog team.

show   **7.** The dog was picked because he had _____ remarkable speed, strength, and courage even as a pup.

draw   **8.** He had _____ heavy sledges hundreds of miles over steep and perilous country.

begin   **9.** With a load of thousands of tiny bottles of antitoxin, Kaasen, Balto, and the dog team _____ the last leg of the journey to Nome.

fall   **10.** A heavy snow had recently _____.

lose   **11.** At two o'clock one morning, in the pitch dark and the biting cold, Kaasen completely _____ his sense of direction in the fury of the blizzard.

freeze   **12.** One side of his face had been _____.

give   **13.** He stopped the team, patted Balto on the head, and confessed to the dog that he had _____ up.

speak   **14.** After his master had _____, Balto sniffed the air and chose his own course.

run   **15.** Fortunately, he still remembered the old trail that he had _____ several times before.

Continued ☞

run **16.** At one point Balto stopped the rest of the dogs before they _____ into icy water.

grow **17.** Some of the dogs had _____ weak.

wear **18.** The effort had _____ them out so much that they had to be carried on the sled.

see **19.** Finally Kaasen _____ tiny specks of light in the distance: Nome!

see **20.** Not long after he had _____ the lights of the town, Kaasen and his team reached their destination.

EXERCISE D Each of the following sentences is written in the passive voice. On the lines provided, rewrite each sentence in the active voice. If the performer of the action is not mentioned, leave the sentence as it is and write *C*.

> EXAMPLE **1.** The police emergency phone is sometimes answered by an officer rather than by the dispatcher. *An officer, rather than the dispatcher, sometimes answers the police emergency phone.*

1. An emergency call from a woman was received by a police officer at station headquarters. ____

_____

_____

2. When her address was reached by the officer, a prowler was discovered in the back yard. _____

_____

_____

3. Several pieces of jewelry were found in the prowler's pockets. _____

_____

4. The jewelry had been stolen by him, the prowler confessed, from an upstairs bedroom. _____

_____

5. The prowler was quickly led away to jail by the police officer. _____

_____

EXERCISE E On the line provided, identify the voice of each of the following sentences by writing *A* for active or *P* for passive.

> EXAMPLE ____*P*____ **1.** Rita Dove was named poet laureate of the United States in 1993.

_____ **1.** Acute observation makes her poetry shine.

_____ **2.** Who hasn't been bitten by an ant?

_____ **3.** Haitians had claimed their independence long ago.

_____ **4.** Additional applications will be accepted until July 1.

_____ **5.** A basket of flowers had been left on the porch.

LANGUAGE HANDBOOK **4** **USING PRONOUNS**

| WORSHEET 1 | ## Using Personal Pronouns in the Nominative Case (Rules 4 a, b) |

EXERCISE A   For each of the following sentences, write an appropriate personal pronoun on the line provided within the sentence. Then, on the line before the sentence, write whether the pronoun is being used as a subject (*S*) or as a predicate nominative (*PN*). Use a variety of pronouns. Do not use *you* or *it*.

EXAMPLE   __*PN*__   **1.** In our family, the chefs are Rick and ____*I*____.

_____   **1.** Gandhi faced ridicule, imprisonment, and death, but _____ remained faithful to his ideals.

_____   **2.** For the third year in a row, the captain of the girl's squad will be _____.

_____   **3.** Writing music is easy for me, but _____ sometimes have difficulty with the lyrics.

_____   **4.** Our party spent the night with relatives in Nairobi; the next day, _____ got our first sight of wild giraffes.

_____   **5.** After ten days at sea, the only survivors were Luke and _____.

_____   **6.** Elena claims to be afraid of heights, but there at the top of the Ferris wheel was _____.

_____   **7.** Had the train not been delayed, _____ would have spoken at the conference.

_____   **8.** As it happened, the only person who had the necessary qualifications was _____.

_____   **9.** The expedition to the pole was arduous, but _____ arrived in triumph.

_____   **10.** "This is _____," my father answered the phone caller.

EXERCISE B   Most of the following sentences contain errors in pronoun usage. Underline each error, and then write the correct pronoun form on the line provided. If a sentence is already correct, write *C*.

EXAMPLE   __*she*__   **1.** Were Elena and <u>her</u> the only ones there?

_____   **1.** Libraries enthralled writer Jorge Luis Borges as a child, so it is no surprise that he became a librarian as well as a writer.

_____   **2.** Should her and Hal attend this meeting as well?

_____   **3.** The one who was more surprised by the joke was me.

_____   **4.** Yes, your honor, Mr. Radley and me were alone at the time.

_____   **5.** Within a year, the leading competitors in the state became Matt and him.

_____   **6.** Standing at the very end of the line were Stan and them.

_____   **7.** The authors who gave me the best understanding of Chinese American culture were Maxine Hong Kingston and her.

_____   **8.** The old man and them watched with trusting eyes.

_____   **9.** Whenever she answers the phone, she always says, "This is her."

_____   **10.** Shouldn't the Drama Club's advisor be Mrs. Jenkins or he?

LANGUAGE
HANDBOOK **4** **USING PRONOUNS**

WORKSHEET 2 | **Using Personal Pronouns in the Objective Case**
(Rules 4 c, d)

EXERCISE A   For each of the following sentences, write an appropriate personal pronoun on the line provided within the sentence. Then, on the line before the sentence, identify the pronoun as a direct object (*DO*), an indirect object (*IO*), or the object of a preposition (*OP*). Use a variety of pronouns. Do not use *you* or *it*.

EXAMPLE _____IO_____ **1.** My little brother told ____me____ all about the animals of the Chinese calendar.

_____ **1.** Some sparrows seem to thank the children and _____ for the birdseed cakes we hung on the trees.

_____ **2.** Gingerly, the unicorn took a tentative step forward and nickered softly to _____.

_____ **3.** The college awarded Ms. Rivera and _____ honorary diplomas.

_____ **4.** My grandfather taught _____ a way to grow crystals.

_____ **5.** At the dinner party, the seats of honor were given to _____.

_____ **6.** The temperature of the cold spring water startled _____.

_____ **7.** Australian Aborigines were not the only ancient peoples to use boomerangs; several other cultures also used _____.

_____ **8.** For now, let's keep this news just between you and _____.

_____ **9.** When Aunt Bev left for Paris, my sister and I gave _____ a shopping list and some money.

_____ **10.** Fax _____ the results as soon as you get them.

EXERCISE B   Most of the following sentences contain errors in pronoun usage. Underline each error. Then, write the correct form on the line provided. If a sentence is already correct, write *C*.

EXAMPLE _____me_____ **1.** The architect built my wife and I the perfect house.

_____ **1.** Save Juan and her a place up front!

_____ **2.** He spoke of how the great James Baldwin inspired he and so many of his contemporaries.

_____ **3.** Will you coach Lucy and we on our lines?

_____ **4.** To Randy and I, the day was just like any other.

_____ **5.** Did you send Mr. Alva and they confirmation for their cabin?

_____ **6.** There's no argument between Harry and I.

_____ **7.** Make my brother and she a piñata that looks like a car, please.

_____ **8.** An intricate wrought-iron fence stood between the garden and he.

Continued ☞

Elements of Literature

_____ **9.** Did you see the look on their faces when we gave Billy and he their presents!

_____ **10.** My brother might lend my sister and I a couple of dollars.

EXERCISE C   Complete each of the following sentences by writing the pronoun described in parentheses.

> **EXAMPLE 1.** Dad has already ordered Mom and ___*you*___ the special. (*second person singular*)

1. How kind of you to remember _____! (*first person singular*)

2. Of course, you can ride with Steven and _____. (*first person plural*)

3. When my sisters and I heard that Maya Angelou was going speak here in town, we had to go and see _____. (*third person singular*)

4. Of course we're bringing a gift for _____! (*third person singular*)

5. Didn't Mr. Murphy offer _____ a videotape of a film based on *The Joy Luck Club*? (*third person plural*)

6. Syd asked _____ to bring stuffed celery to the party. (*first person singular*)

7. Janice showed _____ how to solve the problem. (*third person singular*)

8. Our friends took _____ to the soccer playoff. (*third person plural*)

9. Why didn't he ask _____ to go with him? (*first person plural*)

10. I watched the baby play with _____ for hours. (*third person singular*)

11. Tom couldn't have seen _____ in the crowd. (*second person singular*)

12. Kelly has worked with _____ for four years. (*first person singular*)

13. We elected _____ class president. (*third person singular*)

14. The runners quickly handed _____ the batons. (*third person plural*)

15. Mom asked _____ to finish cleaning the house. (*first person plural*)

16. How many of _____ want to take part in the debate? (*second person plural*)

17. Did you get your book back from _____? (*third person singular*)

18. Shannon, the telephone call is for _____. (*second person singular*)

19. All of _____ in the trumpet section, line up here. (*second person plural*)

20. Darla, please read _____ a story and put them to bed. (*third person plural*)

LANGUAGE HANDBOOK 4 USING PRONOUNS

WORKSHEET 3 | Identifying Correct Pronoun Usage (Rules 4 a–e)

EXERCISE A Underline the correct pronoun(s) in parentheses in each of the following sentences.

> **EXAMPLE 1.** Did Mona or (<u>*she*</u>, *her*) score the first goal?

1. The DeSalvos or (*they, them*) drive the children to school.
2. It was (*they, them*) who blamed us for the collision.
3. "May I speak to Estella?" "This is (*she, her*) speaking."
4. The Feldmans and (*we, us*) belong to the same synagogue.
5. How can you be so sure (*them, their*) leaving caused the party to end?
6. (*She, Her*) and (*I, me*) were the first ones in line.
7. Why couldn't it have been (*us, we*) who won the playoff game?
8. Either Michelle or (*her, she*) should introduce the speaker.
9. If I were (*her, she*), I would insist on an explanation.
10. It was (*him, his*) faithful practicing that ensured his win in the chess tournament.
11. The reporter snapped a picture of (*she, her*) and (*I, me*).
12. Anthony will see you or (*her, she*) about the party plans.
13. Between you and (*I, me*), Mr. James is not a good speaker.
14. There is plenty of room for you and (*me, I*).
15. Bob and (*I, me*) will play against Iris and (*her, she*).
16. Leslie taught (*him, he*) and his sister to drive.
17. Oak Park hasn't beaten Western or (*we, us*) this season.
18. Aunt Dolores took my cousin and (*me, I*) to the aquarium.
19. The car missed Tranh and (*me, I*) by a few inches.
20. They will leave their dog with the Tallchiefs or (*we, us*).

EXERCISE B Underline the pronoun in each of the following sentences. Then, on the line provided, identify its person (*first, second,* or *third*) and number (*singular* or *plural*).

	PERSON	NUMBER
EXAMPLE 1. Class, <u>you</u> did well on these reports.	*second*	*plural*
1. Are we having a reception for the exchange students?	_____	_____
2. Then Ted passed him the ball.	_____	_____
3. Put them in the warehouse.	_____	_____
4. Fireflies flitted in the darkness around me.	_____	_____
5. Shouldn't the captain have been you?	_____	_____

Elements of Literature

| WORSHEET 4 | **Using Pronouns as Appositives and in Elliptical Constructions (Rules 4 f, i)** |

EXERCISE Underline the pronouns in parentheses that are in the correct case.

> **EXAMPLE 1.** After next week's meet, (<u>we</u>, *us*) gymnasts will be finished with the season's competitions.

1. The passing car splashed Luís more than (*I, me*); in fact, my clothes were completely dry.

2. Few people work as hard as (*she, her*).

3. We have attended two more classes than (*they, them*).

4. The Gabers don't have as many expenses as (*we, us*).

5. The dog's constant barking annoyed the Garcías more than (*we, us*) because our thick walls muffle sound.

6. After Don and I had worked hard all week, the restaurant owner paid Don more than (*me, I*).

7. Masako can type more accurately than (*him, he*).

8. Since Jerome always feeds the dog, it obeys him better than (*me, I*), and his cat ignores me, too.

9. Lisa's aunts, Jo Ann and (*she, her*), should offer to help with the dishes.

10. The judge's decision was a complete surprise to two of the spectators, my mother and (*I, me*).

11. Only two students, Brett and (*I, me*), were on corridor duty.

12. Mr. Kramer recognized several juniors, Naomi and (*we, us*), at the last assembly.

13. Two art students, Belinda and (*he, him*), made all the posters.

14. All the posters were made by two students, Bruce and (*her, she*).

15. The two of us, Carmen and (*I, me*), plan to take the course in French literature.

16. The best players in our class, Sandy and (*us, we*), plan to organize a girls' soccer league.

17. The class chose two students, Alice and (*her, she*), to represent them.

18. The library is used by two schools, Evans High and (*we, us*).

19. In a few more weeks, (*we, us*) juniors will become seniors.

20. My two best friends, Janell and (*her, she*), plan to room together in college.

21. The Johnsons live on the same street as (*them, they*).

22. The museum is offering a special discount to (*us, we*) students.

23. The new freeway will benefit Hartford more than (*we, us*) since we seldom drive.

24. The three best students, James, Rebekah and (*I, me*), reviewed for the test together.

25. Only two people, Mr. Muntz and (*she, her*), may sign the building permits.

LANGUAGE HANDBOOK **4** USING PRONOUNS

WORKSHEET 5 Using *Who* and *Whom* (Rule 4 g)

EXERCISE A   Underline the pronoun in parentheses that is correct in formal usage.

> **EXAMPLES 1.** The customer asked to (*who, whom*) the check should be made payable.
>
> **2.** We wanted to know (*who, whom*) was going to ride with us.

1. The boy (*who, whom*) Carlotta asked to the dance gave her a big corsage.

2. The Democrat is the candidate for (*who, whom*) she voted.

3. The Republican is the one (*who, whom*) I think will be elected.

4. The works of Ando Hiroshige, (*who, whom*) is considered the last great master of the Japanese color print, influenced many French Impressionists.

5. Mrs. Gomez asked me if I were the one to (*who, whom*) she owed an apology.

6. Louis Agassiz, (*who, whom*) was one of the greatest geologists, studied the effects of slow-moving fields of ice on the earth's surface.

7. You will have to ask someone (*who, whom*) knows a lot about fishing.

8. Dr. Fowler, (*who, whom*) I respect, does not recommend that medication.

9. The pen pal to (*who, whom*) I have been writing for years is coming to visit me.

10. Naguib Mahfouz, (*who, whom*) I think is a compelling novelist, is among the best-known fiction writers in the Arabic language.

EXERCISE B   Underline the correct pronoun in each set of parentheses in the following paragraph.

> **EXAMPLE [1]** Some people (*who, whom*) think they are invincible often equate adventure and danger.

Are you one of those people [1] (*who, whom*) think that accidents always happen to the other person? The people to [2] (*who, whom*) serious accidents occur seldom expect them. The accident victims about [3] (*who, whom*) we read in the paper did not deliberately plan to get injured. Few drivers [4] (*who, whom*) get into their cars and drive at excessive speeds expect to be the ones [5] (*who, whom*) the police pull out of wrecks. The swimmers [6] (*who, whom*) take unnecessary risks are the ones for [7] (*who, whom*) warnings are useless. It's always the other person [8] (*who, whom*) they suppose gets drowned. Fewer tragedies would occur if people [9] (*who, whom*) take chances would stop to think that they might be the next ones [10] (*who, whom*) misfortune overtakes.

WORKSHEET 6 | Using Reflexive, Intensive, and Possessive Pronouns and Clear Pronoun Reference (Rules 4 e, h, j)

EXERCISE A   For each of the following sentences, draw a line through each error in the use of pronouns. Then, on the line provided, write the correct form of the pronoun. If a sentence is already correct, write *C*.

> EXAMPLE ___*him*___ **1.** Let's introduce Arthur to Annette and ~~himself~~.

_____ **1.** The Antonios and ourselves have lived next to each other in Leestown ever since I can remember.

_____ **2.** Their dad is a brick mason, and he built most of their house himself.

_____ **3.** We recently celebrated us being next-door neighbors for thirteen years.

_____ **4.** Their son Arthur and myself are as close to each other as any brothers could be.

_____ **5.** I really enjoy him having such a goofy sense of humor.

_____ **6.** They have a daughter, Marian. Her having the same birthday as my sister Ellen means we can have one party for both of them.

_____ **7.** Last week, Mr. Antonio got a promotion. The company owner and himself made the announcement together.

_____ **8.** They're now trying to find themselves a house in Madison.

_____ **9.** We are all saddened by them moving to Madison.

_____ **10.** How will Ellen and myself manage without our friends?

EXERCISE B   On the lines provided, revise the following sentences to eliminate unclear pronoun references. While there is more than one way to revise some sentences, you need give only one revision.

> EXAMPLE **1.** When putting the picture in the envelope, I tore it. *I tore the* _____
> *picture when I was putting it in the envelope. or I tore the envelope* _____
> *when I was putting the picture in it.* _____

1. If Mrs. Jackson announces her candidacy, will the local TV station cover it? _____

_____

2. Since the meeting was on the same night as the game, we had to miss it. _____

_____

3. I took the books off the shelves and dusted them. _____

_____

4. If the students are absent, can they make it up? _____

_____

5. Ian couldn't send e-mail to Eddie because he wasn't online. _____

_____

Continued ☞

6. Mom doesn't like Yoki to practice when she is tired. _____

_____

7. When a tooth hurts, find out the reason for it. _____

_____

8. If you find any bugs on the tomato plants, destroy them. _____

_____

9. When the bus left the station, it was practically empty. _____

_____

10. I read *Bury My Heart at Wounded Knee* after I read *Killoyle,* and I really enjoyed it. _____

_____

EXERCISE C   Revise the following sentences to eliminate errors in the use of pronouns.

> EXAMPLE **1.** It's more fun to travel in Japan if you can speak it. *It's more fun to*
> *travel in Japan if you can speak Japanese.*

1. In this movie it shows how traffic accidents occur. _____

_____

2. The Sanchez family fished all day in the Bay of Campeche but didn't catch a single one. _____

_____

3. It says on the sign that swimming there is dangerous. _____

_____

4. As soon as the employees got paid, they deposited them in their bank accounts. _____

_____

5. It shows in the diagram how to put on a life preserver. _____

_____

6. We wanted Denise to bring her mother for a visit when she was in town. _____

_____

7. All the plants are drying up. This is the worst we have ever experienced! _____

_____

8. Does Steve ever borrow David's biology notes after he has studied for a test? _____

_____

9. Finally, the plane arrived at the gate, but they still had to unload the luggage. _____

_____

10. Because I'm not sure which one I might attend after graduation, I am taking various college
admissions tests. _____

_____

LANGUAGE
HANDBOOK **4** **USING PRONOUNS**

WORKSHEET 7 Test (Rules 4 a–j)

EXERCISE A   On the line provided before each of the following sentences, write the correct form of the italicized pronoun. If the pronoun is already correct, write *C*.

> EXAMPLE ___*he*___ **1.** Was it W.E.B. Du Bois or *him* who wrote that collection of essays?

_____ **1.** What was the reason for *him* dropping the course?

_____ **2.** The bouquet of red tulips was from Carlos and *me*.

_____ **3.** If it's *them* at the door, tell them I'll be right out.

_____ **4.** After *who* are the American continents named?

_____ **5.** Joel and *himself* quietly left the room.

_____ **6.** We must play two more schools, Westbrook and *they*.

_____ **7.** The trouble was that Mika could run as fast as *me*.

_____ **8.** *Who* did Lincoln appoint as his secretary of state?

_____ **9.** Do you plan to ride with the Ridleys or *we?*

_____ **10.** Only two students, Wesley and *she,* made perfect scores.

_____ **11.** My parents have no objection to *us* using the basement.

_____ **12.** Jesse and *me* made some popcorn.

_____ **13.** Sabrina and Mario constructed the stage setting *themselves.*

_____ **14.** *Whom* administers the oath of office to the president-elect?

_____ **15.** The long hike had made *we* scouts very hungry.

_____ **16.** There is no reason for *them* raising the price at this time.

_____ **17.** Alma can weld just as well as *him.*

_____ **18.** "Where's the manager?" "That's *her* at the first desk."

_____ **19.** If it was *her*, I certainly didn't recognize her.

_____ **20.** The reporter took my picture without *me* knowing it.

_____ **21.** *Whom* did the anthropologist Ruth Benedict inspire?

_____ **22.** The coach lets Margaret pitch more often than *me;* he probably considers her the star pitcher.

_____ **23.** *Us* students should give full support to our academic and athletic teams.

_____ **24.** Between the bull and *we* stood only a frail wire fence.

_____ **25.** There is nothing wrong with *your* refusing the nomination.

Continued ☞

EXERCISE B   Draw a line through each error in pronoun usage. Then, write the correct form of the pronoun on the line provided. If a sentence is already correct, write *C*.

EXAMPLE ____*l*____ **1.** Many other students and ~~me~~ share a fear of public speaking.

_____ **1.** Several of we students in Mr. Omar's public speaking class were afraid to speak before the group.

_____ **2.** We feel foolish when people laugh at ourselves for making a slight mistake.

_____ **3.** Mr. Omar said that we could overcome our fear if we would only try.

_____ **4.** He told we students who were nervous that we shouldn't object to being laughed at because the laughter was good-natured and friendly.

_____ **5.** He suggested a way by which we could overcome this sensitivity.

_____ **6.** We students would perform some silly stunt before our classmates and, in this way, get used to them laughing at us.

_____ **7.** No one was ever upset by a little laughter after him or her had taken this treatment.

_____ **8.** Two boys—Tony and me—agreed to start.

_____ **9.** It wasn't Tony but me who thought up our idiotic stunt.

_____ **10.** I would gallop around the room like a horse while Tony held onto my shirttail and said, "Giddyap! Giddyap!"

_____ **11.** The idea was that everyone would laugh at him and I and that after that we wouldn't mind being laughed at again.

_____ **12.** Suddenly, in the midst of our act, Sally and Alvin, who were sitting near the door, looked very worried.

_____ **13.** "What's the matter?" I asked, looking at Sally and he.

_____ **14.** "It's the principal herself," gasped Alvin.

_____ **15.** Sure enough, it was her—with a most astonished look on her face.

_____ **16.** When Ms. Hopkins stepped into the room, no one felt sillier than Tony and myself—unless it was our teacher, Mr. Omar.

_____ **17.** The principal looked at we boys, and I could see that she was wondering why on earth we were behaving so crazily.

_____ **18.** "You and he seem to be having a rather lively time," said Ms. Hopkins, who we had never met before.

_____ **19.** "What's wrong with you boys anyway?"

_____ **20.** The principal's sudden entry embarrassed Mr. Omar as much as we.

_____ **21.** It was him who offered the explanation for our peculiar antics.

_____ **22.** "We're having a little lesson in public speaking," he explained to the principal.

_____ **23.** "Speaking?" repeated the principal, who looked more puzzled than ever.

Continued ☞

_____ 24. "Yes, we are trying to help Tony and he overcome their embarrassment," he added.

_____ 25. However, it was plain to see that Mr. Omar was in need of something to overcome his own embarrassment as well as ours.

EXERCISE C   Underline the correct pronoun in parentheses in each of the following sentences.

> **EXAMPLE 1.** (<u>Who</u>, *Whom*) wrote this famous epic poem is still unknown.

1. The newspaper *El Diario* announced (*who, whom*) chose the committee.

2. The newspaper *El Diario* announced (*who, whom*) the committee chose.

3. Scholars have argued about (*who, whom*) wrote Shakespeare's plays.

4. (*Who, Whom*) the president will appoint is anybody's guess.

5. (*Who, Whom*) contributed this money is a secret.

6. The card did not say from (*who, whom*) the flowers came.

7. We finally discovered (*who, whom*) the stranger was.

8. Nobody will envy (*whoever, whomever*) gets this appointment.

9. A prize is given to (*whoever, whomever*) gets the most applause.

10. A prize is given to (*whoever, whomever*) the audience applauds most enthusiastically.

EXERCISE D   Underline the correct pronoun in parentheses in each of the following sentences.

> **EXAMPLE 1.** Maria Tallchief is the dancer (*who*, <u>*whom*</u>) I most admire.

1. Most visitors (*whom, who*) go to Auckland, New Zealand, plan to return someday.

2. Our chief of police is a person (*who, whom*) nobody can intimidate.

3. The witness upon (*whom, who*) the prosecution had been depending failed to appear.

4. People (*whom, who*) flatter you are not necessarily your friends.

5. None of us knew for (*whom, who*) the gift was intended.

6. Edgar Allan Poe is the author (*who, whom*) I believe invented the detective story.

7. My grandmother was a person (*who, whom*) one could never forget.

8. Unclaimed articles are returned to (*whoever, whomever*) turns them in.

9. The people (*who, whom*) I like usually like me.

10. Do you know (*who, whom*) the author of *Cane* is?

Continued ☞

LANGUAGE HANDBOOK 4 WORKSHEET 7 *(continued)*

EXERCISE E On the lines provided, rewrite each sentence so that only one meaning is possible.

> **EXAMPLE 1.** Lily called Annie while she was at work. *While Lily was at work, she called Annie.*

1. I wrote to Frances, but she didn't answer it. _____

_____

_____

2. The shoe store was having a big sale, but I didn't need any at the time. _____

_____

_____

3. Whenever Angelo meets Mr. Gabrielli, he starts to talk about politics. _____

_____

_____

4. If there is jicama in the salad, Uncle Herb will love it. _____

_____

_____

5. Nowadays they insist that you walk soon after most operations. _____

_____

_____

6. How long must you study engineering before you can become one? _____

_____

_____

7. Mrs. Rios told Doba that she had been chosen to participate in the Navajo hoop dance contest.

_____

_____

8. They base grades entirely on tests at that college. _____

_____

_____

9. If your brakes start to slip, you should find out the cause of it. _____

_____

_____

10. A person should get farming experience before buying one. _____

_____

_____

LANGUAGE HANDBOOK **5** **USING MODIFIERS**

WORKSHEET 1	**Using Comparative and Superlative Forms (Rules 5 a, b)**

EXERCISE A For each of the following words, write the comparative and superlative degrees of comparison.

EXAMPLE **1.** certain ____*more certain*____   ____*most certain*____

	Comparative	**Superlative**
1. responsible	_____	_____
2. weary	_____	_____
3. bad	_____	_____
4. dangerous	_____	_____
5. well	_____	_____
6. wildly	_____	_____
7. childish	_____	_____
8. mysteriously	_____	_____
9. close	_____	_____
10. little	_____	_____
11. freely	_____	_____
12. lonely	_____	_____
13. proudly	_____	_____
14. cautiously	_____	_____
15. righteous	_____	_____
16. huge	_____	_____
17. foul	_____	_____
18. far	_____	_____
19. calmly	_____	_____
20. neat	_____	_____
21. hard	_____	_____
22. simple	_____	_____
23. pessimistic	_____	_____
24. big	_____	_____
25. wide	_____	_____

Continued ☞

LANGUAGE HANDBOOK 5 WORSHEET 1 *(continued)*

EXERCISE B   For each of the following sentences, write the modifier in the degree of comparison indicated in parentheses.

> **EXAMPLE** *much* **1.** Each of the triplets wanted to help ___*more*___ than the other. *(comparative)*

light   **1.** Although the bag of foam blocks was almost as big as I was, it was _____ than a roll of quarters. *(comparative)*

bad   **2.** Until the skunk sprayed my dog, I thought that rotten eggs made the _____ smell on earth. *(superlative)*

famous   **3.** In the film industry, the Cannes Film Festival is probably the _____ competition. *(superlative)*

accurate   **4.** Try to make these measurements _____ than the other ones. *(comparative)*

alertly   **5.** I watched the litter for a while; then I chose the puppy that was looking around _____. *(superlative)*

far   **6.** Which planet is _____ from the sun? *(superlative)*

good   **7.** Everybody in town knows that Pappas Restaurant makes the _____ Greek salad around. *(superlative)*

well   **8.** You'll have more energy if you eat _____ than you have been. *(comparative)*

softly   **9.** The dancers moved across the floorboards _____ than the wind. *(comparative)*

less   **10.** That surely had to be the _____ interesting documentary in the library. *(superlative)*

dynamically   **11.** Atoms react _____ in these circumstances. *(superlative)*

pure   **12.** The distilled water tested _____ than either the well water or the bottled water. *(comparative)*

complete   **13.** Roger believed he had a _____ collection of Sherlock Holmes mysteries than anyone else in his reading group. *(comparative)*

feverish   **14.** How much _____ the child seems now. *(comparative)*

wise   **15.** That is the _____ advice I have ever received. *(superlative)*

slowly   **16.** Please cook the vegetables _____ next time. *(comparative)*

expandable   **17.** This section was the _____ of the compartments. *(superlative)*

smart   **18.** Judd proved to be the _____ person in our class. *(superlative)*

grateful   **19.** My grandparents are _____ that they have family nearby. *(positive)*

often   **20.** _____ than not, Robert found that his schedule was easy to manage. *(comparative)*

LANGUAGE HANDBOOK 5 USING MODIFIERS

WORKSHEET 2 | Using Adjectives and Adverbs in Comparison (Rules 5 a–c)

EXERCISE A   For each of the following sentences, draw a line through any incorrect comparison. Then, on the line provided, write the correct comparison. If a sentence is already correct, write *C*.

EXAMPLE _largest_ **1.** The ~~most largest~~ Christian church in the world is St. Peter's Basilica in Rome.

_____ **1.** Janelle's speech was much more original than the others.

_____ **2.** Your handwriting is less neater than your typing.

_____ **3.** To me, nothing is more pleasanter than sailing.

_____ **4.** It was the most neatest room I have ever seen.

_____ **5.** The organic fertilizer has made the grass more greener.

_____ **6.** The Taj Mahal is one of the most beautifullest buildings in existence.

_____ **7.** I have never felt more happier in my entire life.

_____ **8.** This is the most strongest glue that you can buy.

_____ **9.** Modern appliances make housecleaning much more easier.

_____ **10.** These are the least comfortable shoes I have ever worn.

EXERCISE B   Fill in the blank in each of the following sentences by writing the correct form of the word in italics.

EXAMPLE *high* **1.** Angel Falls is __higher__ than Yosemite Falls.

long   **1.** Which is _____, a yard or a meter?

old   **2.** Lee is the _____ of the three sisters.

great   **3.** Was Washington or Lincoln the _____ president?

pretty   **4.** I think that this dress is _____ than the other.

tall   **5.** Nels is the _____ boy in the class.

fast   **6.** Who is the _____ runner, Maria, June, or Tamisha?

far   **7.** The subcompact car ran _____ on a tank of gas than the compact car.

convincing **8.** In the debate, the negative side was _____ than the positive side.

heavy   **9.** Bill's pumpkin was the _____ of all those entered in the county fair.

large   **10.** Asia is the _____ continent in the world.

LANGUAGE HANDBOOK **5** USING MODIFIERS

WORKSHEET 3 | **Revising Double Negatives and Double Comparisons; Making Complete Comparisons (Rules 5 c, d)**

EXERCISE A   Some of the following sentences contain double negatives or double comparisons. On the line provided, write each sentence correctly. If a sentence is already correct, write *C*.

> **EXAMPLE 1.** Can't you talk no louder? _Can you talk louder? or Can't you talk_ _any louder?_

1. Surgeons need the most accuratest measurements possible. _____

_____

2. There weren't none left at the store. _____

_____

3. Nobody can find no Keplars in the phone book. _____

_____

4. They don't know anyone better for the job. _____

_____

5. Which of the jeans did you like more better? _____

_____

EXERCISE B   Most of the following sentences contain incomplete comparisons. On the line provided, revise each sentence. If a sentence is correct, write *C*.

> **EXAMPLE 1.** August feels hotter than all the months. _August feels hotter than_ _all the other months._

1. I understand Stephen Crane's stories better than any stories we've read. _____

_____

2. Keith can type faster than anyone in his class. _____

_____

3. Well, I still think he jumps higher than anybody in the league. _____

_____

4. Alaska is larger than any other state in the United States. _____

_____

5. Is New York really better than any place on earth? _____

_____

| WORSHEET 4 | Correcting Misplaced Modifiers and Avoiding Faulty Comparisons (Rules 5 d–f) |

EXERCISE A Underline each misplaced modifier, and rewrite the sentence with the modifier correctly placed.

EXAMPLE **1.** We <u>only</u> saw the last act of *Miss Saigon*. <u>We saw only the last act of Miss Saigon.</u>

1. Every part is thoroughly tested that goes into a plane. _____

_____

2. The book was about the traditions of the Aborigines that I read last week. _____

_____

_____

3. I found a ticket for the football game to be played in the school lunchroom next Friday. _____

_____

_____

4. My father has been urging me to become a dentist every day. _____

_____

5. Cyril had thrown the magazine into the trash that I needed for my civics class. _____

_____

_____

6. Leon glued together the vase that he had broken very carefully. _____

_____

7. Raquel described the forest fire in her English class she had seen. _____

_____

8. The plane was taken for investigation to the factory where it had been made after the crash.__

_____

_____

9. Teresa couldn't say goodbye to her uncle, Roberto, who was leaving for Chile because of her measles. _____

_____

_____

10. Dr. Chung came here to perform acupuncture from across the state. _____

_____

_____

Continued ☞

LANGUAGE HANDBOOK 5 WORKSHEET 4 *(continued)*

EXERCISE B   Revise the following sentences to make the comparisons logical and clear. If a sentence is already correct, write *C*.

> **EXAMPLE 1.** The woodpecker's bill is longer than the cardinal. *The woodpecker's bill is longer than the cardinal's.*

1. Its bite is as poisonous as a rattlesnake. _____

_____

_____

2. Nina's record is as good as any employee in the company. _____

_____

_____

3. Humans' brains are larger in proportion to their bodies than whales. _____

_____

_____

4. Asia has a greater population than any continent in the world. _____

_____

_____

5. Of all the rodents in the world, rats have caused the most destruction. _____

_____

_____

6. Death Valley is lower than any place in the United States. _____

_____

_____

7. Russia is the largest of any other country in the world. _____

_____

_____

8. Brazil has a greater area than any country in South America. _____

_____

_____

9. Mr. Shapiro likes his cat more than any animal. _____

_____

_____

10. The car dealer made Mom a better offer than he made anyone else. _____

_____

_____

LANGUAGE HANDBOOK 5 USING MODIFIERS

WORKSHEET 5 | **Recognizing Misplaced and Dangling Modifiers (Rules 5 f, g)**

EXERCISE For each of the following pairs of sentences, write the letter of the sentence that does not contain a dangling or misplaced modifier.

EXAMPLES ____*b*____ 1. (a) Together, anything can be done.

(b) Together, we can do anything.

____*a*____ 2. (a) After arriving early, Terry helped to set up the chairs.

(b) After arriving early, the chairs were set up by Terry.

_____ 1. (a) When carefully mended, this tear in Mona's sari will hardly be noticeable.

(b) When carefully mended, you will hardly notice this tear in Mona's sari.

_____ 2. (a) Roasted for four hours, we found the cabrito very tender.

(b) Roasted for four hours, the cabrito was very tender.

_____ 3. (a) Being a light sleeper, the noise awoke my mom.

(b) Being a light sleeper, my mom was awakened by the noise.

_____ 4. (a) If packed in ice, the fish will keep for several days.

(b) If packed in ice, you can keep the fish for several days.

_____ 5. (a) While reading silently, your lips should not move.

(b) While reading silently, you should not move your lips.

_____ 6. (a) Thrifty, Yolanda saves considerable money.

(b) Thrifty, considerable money can be saved.

_____ 7. (a) Piled one on top of the other, the ruins of seven cities were discovered at Hissarlik, Turkey.

(b) Piled one on top of the other, archaeologists discovered the ruins of seven cities at Hissarlik, Turkey.

_____ 8. (a) Needing expert legal advice, Ms. Taosie was consulted by my father.

(b) Needing expert legal advice, my father consulted Ms. Taosie.

_____ 9. (a) To be a successful salesperson, you need a good personality.

(b) To be a successful salesperson, a good personality is needed.

_____ 10. (a) When inflated with air, six people can be carried on the raft.

(b) When inflated with air, the raft can carry six people.

Continued ☞

_____ 11. (a) When training a dog, the same words should always be used.

(b) When training a dog, you should always use the same words.

_____ 12. (a) Though written for children, *Lives of the Writers* is enjoyed by adults.

(b) Though written for children, adults also enjoy *Lives of the Writers.*

_____ 13. (a) Flying over the Indian Ocean, hundreds of islands could be seen.

(b) Flying over the Indian Ocean, we could see hundreds of islands.

_____ 14. (a) To pick the fruit, Wen Fu needed a long ladder.

(b) To pick the fruit, a long ladder was needed by Wen Fu.

_____ 15. (a) Questioned about the check, she answered very evasively.

(b) Questioned about the check, her answers were very evasive.

_____ 16. (a) In selling goods, questions are often asked of the salesclerk.

(b) In selling goods, the salesclerk must often answer questions.

_____ 17. (a) Being easy to forget, a foreign language must be spoken regularly.

(b) Being easy to forget, you must speak a foreign language regularly.

_____ 18. (a) If neatly written, they will give your letter more attention.

(b) If neatly written, your letter will get more attention.

_____ 19. (a) Keeping time to the music, the Mexican hat dance was performed by Juanita.

(b) Keeping time to the music, Juanita performed the Mexican hat dance.

_____ 20. (a) If raised in large quantities, the hungry people of the world could be fed with soybeans.

(b) If raised in large quantities, soybeans could feed the hungry people of the world.

_____ 21. (a) Did Arthur find the fruit he wanted in the refrigerator for lunch?

(b) Did Arthur find the fruit he wanted for lunch in the refrigerator?

_____ 22. (a) Shelley called her parents to let them only know she had passed her final exam.

(b) Shelley called her parents only to let them know she had passed her final exam.

_____ 23. (a) The bagels with the cream cheese were so delicious that they vanished quickly.

(b) The bagels were so delicious that they vanished quickly with the cream cheese.

_____ 24. (a) Because of the sun's heat, I use a reflective screen in the front window in my car.

(b) I use a reflective screen because of the sun's heat in the front window in my car.

_____ 25. (a) We were able to enjoy snorkeling and seeing the fish wearing our face masks.

(b) Wearing our face masks, we were able to enjoy snorkeling and seeing the fish.

Elements of Literature

LANGUAGE HANDBOOK **5**	USING MODIFIERS

WORKSHEET 6	Repairing Dangling Modifiers (Rule 5 g)

EXERCISE A   Revise the following sentences by giving each dangling modifier a word or words to modify.

> EXAMPLE **1.** By reversing the jacket, it can be worn as a raincoat. _By reversing the jacket, you can wear it as a raincoat._

1. To learn to speak Hebrew, much practice is needed. _____

_____

2. Turning on the hose, the sprinkler drenched me. _____

_____

3. Printed in large letters, my attention was attracted. _____

_____

4. Having grown up in West Virginia, coal mines were familiar to me. _____

_____

5. If lost in the woods, your compass can be used to help find your way. _____

_____

EXERCISE B   Revise the following sentences by adding a word or words to the dangling modifier or by rewording the sentence.

> EXAMPLE **1.** While waiting for a bus, a passing car splashed mud on me. _While I was waiting for a bus, a passing car splashed mud on me._

1. If properly chilled, everyone will enjoy this flan. _____

_____

2. Hiking through the underbrush, the camper's clothes were badly torn. _____

_____

_____

3. When in India, your head should be protected from the hot sun. _____

_____

_____

4. Considered a shy, quiet person, Bert's fiery speech astonished everyone. _____

_____

_____

5. While writing my report, my baby sister kept disturbing me. _____

_____

_____

LANGUAGE HANDBOOK 5 USING MODIFIERS

WORKSHEET 7 Test (Rules 5 a–g)

EXERCISE A   For each of the following words, write the comparative and superlative degrees of comparison.

EXAMPLE **1.** complex _____more complex_____   _____most complex_____

	Comparative	**Superlative**
1. clear	_____	_____
2. many	_____	_____
3. enthusiastically	_____	_____
4. narrow	_____	_____
5. optimistic	_____	_____
6. foolish	_____	_____
7. precisely	_____	_____
8. fair	_____	_____
9. fond	_____	_____
10. near	_____	_____

EXERCISE B   In each of the following sentences, underline the correct modifier in parentheses.

EXAMPLE **1.** Of the two films, I found this one (<u>*more*</u>, *most*) enjoyable.

1. This is a (*safer, safest*) model than many on the market.

2. Jamaican music is one of the (*more, most*) upbeat sounds around.

3. There's (*not hardly, hardly*) any left!

4. The teacher always rewarded the child who entered the room (*more quietly, most quietly*).

5. That is the (*most quickest, quickest*) way there.

6. None of us have (*ever, never*) been out of the country.

7. I can't decide which of the five soldiers was (*braver, the bravest*).

8. The three-year-old handled the chicks (*less gently, least gently*) of all the children.

9. After we tried the new knife sharpener, our knives were actually (*less sharp, less sharper*).

10. Please sit down; I (*can, can't*) barely see.

11. Doesn't Australia have the (*most, mostest*) marsupials of any continent?

12. It was the (*less, least*) solemn occasion in my memory.

13. Do you feel (*better, more better*) now?

14. Why aren't there (*any, no*) snakes in Ireland or New Zealand?

Continued ☞

15. Is that the *(worse, worst)* thing that could happen?

16. I can't remember a *(foggier, foggiest)* morning.

17. For years, the Tasmanian devil was *(nowhere, not nowhere)* to be seen.

18. You'll play *(better, best)* tomorrow if you practice more today.

19. Why do you always choose the *(less, least)* ripe banana at the grocery store?

20. The one on page 43 is a *(more harder, harder)* puzzle.

EXERCISE C   In the following sentences, draw a line through incorrectly used modifiers. Then, on the line provided, write the correct form of the modifier. Some sentences also may require an additional word; other sentences without incorrect modifiers may require only an additional word. If a sentence is already correct, write *C.*

EXAMPLE   _darker_   **1.** Is indigo or navy ~~darkest~~?

_____   **1.** Who is tallest, you or your brother?

_____   **2.** That was one of the better productions of *A Raisin in the Sun* that I've ever seen.

_____   **3.** A few years ago, no one in the scientific community believed the rare, elusive bird still existed.

_____   **4.** My dad says that Aretha Franklin sings better than anyone.

_____   **5.** Is Santa Barbara, Reno, or Phoenix closer to us?

_____   **6.** Which of these countries has more cars than any nation in the world?

_____   **7.** Gee, your cold seems worser today.

_____   **8.** Which was greatest, the profit or the expenses?

_____   **9.** Why do you wear the most loosest clothes you can find?

_____   **10.** Doesn't nobody have a set of jumper cables?

EXERCISE D   Most of the following sentences contain illogical comparisons or misplaced or dangling modifiers. On the lines provided, revise each sentence to correct the error. If a sentence is already correct, write *C.*

EXAMPLE **1.** To have a stellar career, education is essential. _Education is_
essential to having a stellar career.

1. Each student taking the test should only have a pencil on his or her desk. _____

_____

_____

2. Dazzled, the sun was momentarily blinding. _____

_____

_____

Continued ☞

3. Her beauty is envied more than any other woman. _____

_____

_____

4. When painting wood, primer should be applied first. _____

_____

_____

5. Tourists enjoy our lifestyle more than any other city. _____

_____

_____

6. Camels carried heavy packs plodding tirelessly over the sand. _____

_____

_____

7. Terrified, the chickens squawked as the fox prowled nearby. _____

_____

_____

8. I think the traffic in Houston is worse than Atlanta. _____

_____

_____

9. Mystified, every circuit seemed in order, yet the computer would not turn on. _____

_____

_____

10. Home at last, trouble seemed far away. _____

_____

_____

EXERCISE E   Each sentence in this story of "Wrong-Way" Corrigan's sensational flight contains an error in the use of modifiers. Rewrite each sentence correctly on the lines provided.

EXAMPLE 1. This is the story of an airplane flight that was probably more unusual than any flight in the history of aviation. *This is the story of an airplane flight that was probably more unusual than any other flight in the history of aviation.*

1. Douglas Corrigan worked on a plane in a California airplane factory that Lindbergh had ordered for his flight to Paris. _____

_____

_____

Continued ☞

LANGUAGE HANDBOOK 5 WORKSHEET 7 *(continued)*

2. After Lindbergh's famous flight, the idea of making a solo flight across the Atlantic came to Corrigan. _____

_____

_____

3. With this solo flight in mind, an old Curtiss Robin airplane was purchased for $310 by Corrigan. _____

_____

_____

4. With its engine overhauled, Corrigan flew the plane nonstop from Long Beach, California, to New York. _____

_____

_____

5. Corrigan applied for permission to fly across the Atlantic several times, but his applications were always turned down. _____

_____

_____

6. After being overhauled, he filed a flight plan to take his plane on a nonstop flight back from New York to Los Angeles. _____

_____

_____

7. In taking off for his return to California, a faulty compass caused Corrigan to turn east instead of west. _____

_____

_____

8. After flying for twenty-nine hours, the coast of Ireland could be seen. _____

_____

_____

9. Without a map, Corrigan had crossed the great Atlantic in a flying jalopy inferior to Lindbergh.

_____

_____

10. On Corrigan's return to the United States, the mayor of one city gave a watch to "Wrong-Way" Corrigan whose hands traveled backward. _____

_____

_____

LANGUAGE HANDBOOK **6** **PHRASES**

| WORKSHEET 1 | Identifying Prepositional Phrases (Rules 6 a, b) |

EXERCISE A   In each of the following sentences, identify the italicized phrase as an adjective phrase (*ADJ*) or an adverb phrase (*ADV*) on the line provided.

EXAMPLES   ___ADV___   **1.** Sand paintings created *by American Indians* are amazing.

___ADJ___   **2.** Is he the best candidate *for that office*?

_____   **1.** Countee Cullen's poetry makes simple but strong statements *about racism*.

_____   **2.** *Throughout his life* he worked hard writing, editing, and teaching.

_____   **3.** They cooked the meal *inside the house* but ate outside.

_____   **4.** She took it *upon herself* to use real dishes, to save paper.

_____   **5.** The view *between the mountains* is especially scenic.

_____   **6.** Don't look *behind that door*!

_____   **7.** The pan of enchiladas is too hot to be set on the table *without a hot pad*.

_____   **8.** The first island *beyond the breakers* has a wonderful beach.

_____   **9.** Our letters *to the city council* helped them decide to support a teen club.

_____   **10.** The directions *below the warning label* tell how to use the wrench.

EXERCISE B   In each of the following sentences, underline each preposition once and each object of the preposition twice. On the line provided, tell whether the prepositional phrase is an adverb phrase (*ADV*) or an adjective phrase (*ADJ*).

EXAMPLE   ___ADV___   **1.** The wind is blowing <u>from</u> the <u>north</u>.

_____   **1.** Santa Fe, which means "holy faith," is the capital of New Mexico.

_____   **2.** "Have you looked in the encyclopedia?" asked Azami.

_____   **3.** "It didn't have enough information about Ralph Waldo Emerson," Janna said.

_____   **4.** "Several friends and I correspond by e-mail," Morgan said.

_____   **5.** It seems that e-mail is the preferred way of communication now.

_____   **6.** The president of the corporation was once the company secretary.

_____   **7.** The Spanish class is planning a trip across Mexico next spring.

_____   **8.** Old Faithful geyser is within Yellowstone National Park.

_____   **9.** Under the willow tree huddled the horses.

_____   **10.** The art was produced through Japanese printmaking techniques.

LANGUAGE HANDBOOK 6 PHRASES

WORKSHEET 2 | **Identifying Participles and Participial Phrases (Rules 6 a, c)**

EXERCISE A   In each of the following sentences, underline the word or words modified by the italicized participle or participial phrase.

> EXAMPLE **1.** The <u>branch</u>, *blowing in the wind*, cast strange shadows on my window.

1. Karen Blixen, *using the name Isak Dinesen*, wrote both fiction and nonfiction.

2. *Watching them warily*, the bobcat moved softly across the field.

3. Dave's parents, *overjoyed by his success*, gave a celebration party.

4. Lorraine Hansberry, *writing about African American life*, created the prize-winning play <u>A Raisin in the Sun.</u>

5. *Jumping from tree to tree*, the squirrel seemed to fly.

6. *Reviewing my notes*, I noticed an error in logic.

7. *Angered by the disturbance*, the bull ran toward the trespassers.

8. *Writing and speaking eloquently*, Dr. Martin Luther King, Jr., inspired generations.

9. We could smell the pizza *burning*.

10. My very tall brother, *disgusted about being asked if he plays basketball*, answers, "No, do you play miniature golf?"

EXERCISE B   In each of the following sentences, underline each participle or participial phrase once and underline the word it modifies twice.

> EXAMPLE **1.** <u>Swimming close to shore</u>, the <u>porpoises</u> attracted many watchers.

1. The puppies, crying from loneliness, watched for their mother.

2. Left for too long, they began to climb out of their box.

3. The basmati rice, steamed to perfection, was delicious with the curry.

4. Writing about Vietnam, Yusef Komunyakaa, a poet from Louisiana, is unflinchingly candid.

5. Knowing the meanings of clouds, my grandfather accurately predicts the weather.

6. Writing *The Natural*, his first novel, Bernard Malamud focused on baseball.

7. Charmed by the kitten, she offered it some milk.

8. As the bus pulled away, we saw several people waving.

9. The fern, grown in the tropics, did not do well in the Adirondacks.

10. Their trip to El Paso, taken on horseback, lasted two weeks.

LANGUAGE HANDBOOK **6** **PHRASES**

WORSHEET 3 | **Identifying Gerunds and Gerund Phrases**
(Rules 6 a, d)

EXERCISE A Underline the gerunds in the following sentences. On the line provided, identify each gerund by writing *S* for subject, *DO* for direct object, *IO* for indirect object, *PN* for predicate nominative, or *OP* for object of a preposition.

EXAMPLES _DO_ **1.** Do you like <u>hiking</u>?

_PN, PN_ **2.** Dan's favorite activities are <u>camping</u> and <u>fishing</u>.

_____ **1.** Wyatt learned television repair through taking correspondence courses.

_____ **2.** Batini enjoys wearing kente-cloth skirts.

_____ **3.** Walking daily is an excellent habit to acquire.

_____ **4.** In fact, I give walking my highest recommendation.

_____ **5.** One way of helping the environment is by recycling everything possible.

_____ **6.** Traveling through the Navajo lands in Arizona can be a thrilling experience.

_____ **7.** My uncle Buck's surprise was his successfully riding a zebra he had trained.

_____ **8.** We enjoy hearing Count Basie's jazz on old records.

_____ **9.** A simple way to please a dog is playing its favorite games.

_____ **10.** Mando gives rock climbing a top priority.

EXERCISE B Complete each of the following phrases or sentences by adding a gerund or gerund phrase that serves the function indicated in parentheses.

EXAMPLES **1.** My very dramatic brother enjoys (*direct object*). _My very_
dramatic brother enjoys performing.

2. My hobby is (*predicate nominative*). _My hobby is writing poetry._

1. Paloma gave (*indirect object*) her total concentration. _____

_____

2. (*subject*) is fun if you like the ocean. _____

_____

3. Julio's favorite part of baseball is (*predicate nominative*). _____

_____

4. My Mexican aunt taught me (*direct object*). _____

_____

5. You need to use caution in (*object of the preposition*). _____

_____

Continued ☞

6. When Toshiko is tired, (*subject*) usually revives him. _____

_____

7. The cats enjoy (*direct object*). _____

_____

8. My uncle made a career of (*object of the preposition*). _____

_____

9. The first order of business is (*predicate nominative*). _____

_____

10. The Belgian sheepdog gave (*indirect object*) his full attention. _____

_____

11. Do you think Ms. Sanford would explain (*direct object*) to us one more time? _____

_____

12. My brother and I resolve problems by (*object of preposition*). _____

_____

13. Harriet's first job each day is (*predicate nominative*). _____

_____

14. Why does Jeffrey practice (*direct object*) every day after school? _____

_____

15. After her night classes, Keesha's best skill became (*predicate nominative*). _____

_____

16. Give (*indirect object*) a higher priority in your schedule! _____

_____

17. Because of (*object of preposition*), we boarded up the windows. _____

_____

18. Allan thought that (*subject*) should be what we did next. _____

_____

19. At the end of a section of stitches, Aunt Clara gives (*indirect object*) a quick review.

_____

_____

20. (*subject*) around the track is the best way I have found to cool down after I run laps.

_____

_____

WORKSHEET 4 | **Identifying and Using Infinitives, Infinitive Phrases, and Infinitive Clauses (Rules 6 a, e, f)**

EXERCISE A   Underline the infinitive, infinitive phrase, or infinitive clause in each sentence. On the line provided, tell whether it is used as a noun (*N*), an adjective (*ADJ*), or an adverb (*ADV*). If the infinitive is used as a noun, indicate whether it is a subject (*S*), a direct object (*DO*), or a predicate nominative (*PN*). If the infinitive is used as an adjective or adverb, underline the word modified twice. If the infinitive is used in an infinitive clause, identify it as *CL* on the line.

EXAMPLES _____ADV_____ **1.** They <u>ran</u> <u>to meet their grandparents</u>.

_____N, S_____ **2.** <u>To get rich</u> would be exciting.

_____N, DO,CL_____ **3.** The director wants <u>us to start the scene from the beginning</u>.

_____ **1.** The workout required us to stretch our bodies.

_____ **2.** Our main goal is to keep the roadsides clean.

_____ **3.** To plant a tree is an act of hope.

_____ **4.** Edgar Allan Poe's eerie stories have the power to disturb readers.

_____ **5.** The poetry to memorize is Langston Hughes's.

_____ **6.** Javier forgot to bring his photographs of surfing.

_____ **7.** We expected her to give the exam on Thursday.

_____ **8.** To save abandoned animals is Adowa's cause.

_____ **9.** My goal as a dancer is to learn flamenco.

_____ **10.** We went to the concert to hear folk music.

EXERCISE B   Complete each of the following phrases or sentences by adding an infinitive, infinitive phrase, or infinitive clause that serves the function indicated in parentheses.

EXAMPLE **1.** I have plans (*adjective*). _I have plans to go to a vocational school._

1. With a cheerful smile she started (*direct object*). _____

_____

2. The long-range goal is (*predicate nominative*). _____

_____

3. (*subject*) is my long-term goal. _____

_____

4. The abstract painting is the one (*adjective*). _____

_____

5. The contest forms direct (*direct object, infinitive clause*). _____

_____

Continued ☞

6. When our house burned, the neighbors offered (*direct object*). _____

_____

7. (*subject*) was all that I needed that day. _____

_____

8. The raccoon was able (*adverb*). _____

_____

9. This is the car (*adjective*). _____

_____

10. The elephant's search was (*predicate nominative*). _____

_____

11. Before the awards ceremony began, the principal prompted (*direct object, infinitive clause*).

_____

_____

12. (*adverb*), you should leave here in about an hour. _____

_____

13. Let us know whether this job is (*predicate nominative*). _____

_____

14. I believe that Julia wants (*direct object*) in the fall. _____

_____

15. (*subject*) requires a great deal of planning. _____

_____

16. Meet the first astronaut who was chosen (*adverb*)! _____

_____

17. Phil is always looking for the best places (*adjective*). _____

_____

18. The hairstylist tried (*direct object*). _____

_____

19. Knowing that we were going to the concert, Moira begged (*direct object, infinitive clause*).

_____

_____

20. (*subject*) is quite an honor. _____

_____

WORSHEET 5 | **Identifying and Using Appositives and Appositive Phrases (Rules 6 a, g)**

EXERCISE A   Underline the appositive or appositive phrase in each sentence below. Underline twice the word or words to which it refers.

> **EXAMPLE 1.** Jin and his sister Akako are visiting relatives in Japan.

1. Machu Picchu, the ancient Inca city, is high in the Andes Mountains.

2. George Washington Carver, a plant scientist, discovered many uses for peanuts.

3. My favorite form of peanuts, peanut butter, is always on hand.

4. Yangon, the capital of Myanmar, is a very large city.

5. Halibut, flat-bodied fish, live in the northern Pacific and Atlantic oceans.

6. Formerly a private estate, the park is now open to the public.

7. Formidable predators, owls help keep a balance in nature.

8. Pacifists, people who oppose war, support diplomacy as a way of ending disputes.

9. Receiving scholarships to MIT are Bonita and Keung, the top science students.

10. Eggplant, a favorite Middle Eastern food, is delicious in salads and vegetable stews.

EXERCISE B   On the lines provided, combine each of the following pairs of sentences by forming an appositive or appositive phrase from one of the sentences.

> **EXAMPLE 1.** Mike is an art director for television sitcoms. Mike is my brother.
> *My brother Mike is an art director for television sitcoms.*
> *or*
> *Mike, an art director for television sitcoms, is my brother.*

1. Mr. Alp enjoys eating tuna fish. Mr. Alp is our sixteen-year-old cat. _____

_____

_____

2. Detroit, Michigan, is the headquarters of several major automobile companies. It was also the original home of Motown Records. _____

_____

_____

3. *The Big Sleep* is playing on television this weekend. It is one of my favorite movies. _____

_____

_____

Continued ☞

4. Easter Island is the home of the striking statues known as *moai*. Easter Island is a small, remote island in the Pacific Ocean. _____

_____

_____

_____

5. George Frideric Handel is the composer of the *Messiah*. The *Messiah* is an oratorio. _____

_____

_____

_____

6. English is the class I will miss the most. English is taught by my favorite teacher. _____

_____

_____

_____

7. Emily Dickinson is a well-known American poet. She is the author of "Tell all the Truth but tell it slant." _____

_____

_____

_____

8. Ennio Morricone has written the music for many films. He is an Italian composer. _____

_____

_____

_____

9. The new playground is a popular place for neighborhood children. The playground is the one with the wooden playscape. _____

_____

_____

_____

10. Tom is a civil engineer for the highway department. He is interested in railroads. _____

_____

_____

_____

LANGUAGE HANDBOOK **6** **PHRASES**

WORKSHEET 6 Test (Rules 6 a–g)

EXERCISE A   In each of the following sentences, underline the prepositional phrase once and the word or words the phrase modifies twice. Then, on the line provided, identify the phrase by writing *ADJ* for adjective phrase or *ADV* for adverb phrase.

>   **EXAMPLE**   ___ADV___   **1.** The doctor said, "Eat an apple and <u>call</u> me <u>in the morning</u>."

_____   **1.** The hot-air balloon fiesta in Albuquerque, New Mexico, is a popular event.

_____   **2.** Balloons of every shape and size can be seen there.

_____   **3.** Balloons may be observed from the balloon park or other city areas.

_____   **4.** Some people drive up Sandia Mountain to watch the balloons ascend.

_____   **5.** The mountain overlook gives them an eye-level view of the rising balloons.

EXERCISE B   On the line provided, identify the italicized phrase in each of the following sentences. Write *PREP* for prepositional phrase or *PART* for participial phrase. Then, underline the word or words each phrase modifies. Do not separately identify a prepositional phrase that is part of a participial phrase.

>   **EXAMPLES**   ___PART___   **1.** <u>Lola</u>, *excited to be at the observatory*, was intrigued by the large telescope.
>
>   ___PREP___   **2.** On the bus, Tara <u>looked</u> *for her friend Kimi.*

_____   **1.** People gazing at the night sky developed the science *of astronomy.*

_____   **2.** Astronomers, *continuing the oldest science*, still make discoveries.

_____   **3.** Ancient Babylonians, Egyptians, and Greeks developed theories *about the universe.*

_____   **4.** One of these theories, *elaborated by Aristotle*, was that earth is the center of the universe.

_____   **5.** *Knowing the location of heavenly bodies*, the Aztecs and Mayans planned the right time to plant crops.

_____   **6.** The Aztecs built massive pyramids dedicated *to the sun and moon.*

_____   **7.** *Fascinated by the heavens*, people through the ages observed and recorded astronomical information.

_____   **8.** Astronomers today, *using sophisticated equipment*, can see deeper into space than ever before.

_____   **9.** Many ordinary people, *awed by the night sky*, have made wishes on falling stars.

_____   **10.** How many more mysteries of space will be discovered *in our lifetimes*?

Continued ☞

EXERCISE C   On the line provided, identify each italicized phrase or clause in the following sentences as *PREP* for prepositional phrase, *PART* for participial phrase, *INF* for infinitive phrase, *CL* for infinitive clause, *GER* for gerund phrase, or *APP* for appositive phrase. Do not separately identify a prepositional phrase that is part of a larger phrase.

EXAMPLE   _GER_   **1.** Bernadette liked *reading about ladybugs.*

_____ **1.** *Celebrating the sixteenth of September* is a tradition in Mexico.

_____ **2.** *To find a good summer job* is the goal of everyone in the class.

_____ **3.** The peach orchard is located two miles *outside the city limits.*

_____ **4.** This was Maura's first trip to Canada, *home of the maple leaf flag.*

_____ **5.** Eliza heard something *scratching on the back window of her car.*

_____ **6.** Crandall's new hobby is *collecting different colored seashells.*

_____ **7.** The bus driver required *them to refrain from yelling.*

_____ **8.** The Iroquois lived *in sturdy wooden longhouses.*

_____ **9.** The Irish setter, *my favorite,* won at the dog show.

_____ **10.** The concert tour dates *listed in the paper* were incorrect.

_____ **11.** This morning Mom ordered *me to straighten up my room.*

_____ **12.** *Consumed with joy,* the winners hugged everyone in sight.

_____ **13.** The movie *to see this holiday season* is It's a Wonderful Life.

_____ **14.** The Asian American Club was sponsor *of the school's first diversity workshop.*

_____ **15.** The parking attendant instructed *us to drive across the roof.*

_____ **16.** The security guard *making his nightly rounds* spied the groundhog babies.

_____ **17.** Annamaria has a talent for *skating on thin ice in a discussion.*

_____ **18.** Ivan walked through the woods *to locate edible mushrooms.*

_____ **19.** *During the next semester* we will study authors of the Harlem Renaissance.

_____ **20.** Troy, *the new boy in class,* wants to become a chef.

_____ **21.** Next week, we expect *Elaine to return from her vacation.*

_____ **22.** *Amazed by the large crowd of friends,* Greg enjoyed his birthday party.

_____ **23.** Through the winter months, the deer search everywhere *to find food.*

_____ **24.** *Reading for fun* seemed to be the theme of every booth we visited.

_____ **25.** Hannah found the Internet addresses *listed on the back cover.*

Continued ☞

EXERCISE D   Label each of the ten italicized verbals in the following paragraph by writing *INF* for infinitive, *GER* for gerund, *PAST PART* for past participle, or *PRES PART* for present participle.

> **EXAMPLE 1.** We often hear people *blaming* [1] _PRES PART_ others for their own misdeeds.

There is a natural tendency in all of us *to blame* [1] _____ others for our mistakes instead of *taking* [2] _____ responsibility for ourselves. *Attempting* [3] _____ *to lessen* [4] _____ our painful sense of guilt as we look at a *broken* [5] _____ dish, we accuse another of *causing* [6] _____ the disaster by *placing* [7] _____ the object too near the edge of the table. We, *regaining* [8] _____ our senses, are finally willing *to take* [9] _____ responsibility for the mishap *caused* [10] _____ by our own carelessness.

EXERCISE E On the lines provided, complete each sentence with the type of phrase or clause indicated in parentheses.

1. By next month, Andrew hopes to stop (*gerund phrase*). _____
   _____

2. How soon does Coach want (*infinitive clause*)? _____
   _____

3. Our field trip (*adjective prepositional phrase*) lasted all morning. _____
   _____

4. (*present participial phrase*), the reporters gathered in the briefing room. _____
   _____

5. Then, Teresa asked her parents if it was time (*infinitive*). _____
   _____

6. Each of the photographs (*past participial phrase*) brought back a delightful memory. _____
   _____

7. Jennifer looked forward to seeing her relatives, (*appositive phrase*). _____
   _____

8. (*present participial phrase*), Charlie began to look for a place to pitch camp. _____
   _____

9. By the end of the summer, we were ready (*infinitive phrase*). _____
   _____

10. (*adverb prepositional phrase*), Deborah's science project won first place. _____

LANGUAGE HANDBOOK 7 CLAUSES

| WORKSHEET 1 | Identifying and Using Independent and Subordinate Clauses (Rules 7 a–c) |

EXERCISE A On the line provided, label each independent clause *I* and each subordinate clause *S*.

　　　　　EXAMPLES ___*S*___ **1.** whom we visited in Manila

　　　　　　　　　　___*I*___ **2.** anyone may join

_____ **1.** after we had eaten supper

_____ **2.** everyone has feelings

_____ **3.** if she could reach the tiller

_____ **4.** then she began to cry

_____ **5.** afterward we ate supper

_____ **6.** now I understand

_____ **7.** although the economist had predicted

_____ **8.** whose car Latisha learned to drive

_____ **9.** which never opens on Sunday

_____ **10.** that book is interesting

EXERCISE B Add an independent clause to each of the following subordinate clauses to create a complete sentence.

　　　　EXAMPLE **1.** after I saw the movie *Titanic* *I became interested in shipbuilding*
　　　　　　　　after I saw the movie Titanic.

1. that I ordered from the catalog _____

_____

2. whose mother was born in Portugal _____

_____

3. because the pickup truck is out of gas _____

_____

4. when the cotton gin is purchased by the cooperative _____

_____

5. even though we were worried about a drought _____

_____

LANGUAGE HANDBOOK 7 CLAUSES

WORKSHEET 2 Identifying Adjective Clauses (Rule 7 d)

EXERCISE A   Underline each adjective clause in the following sentences. Then, draw an arrow to the word or words modified by the adjective clause.

> **EXAMPLE 1.** Colors have symbolic significance of which we are not always aware.

1. Green, for instance, is a color that reminds us of vegetation.

2. The green man who sometimes appears on inn signs in England commemorates an important figure in old springtime festivities.

3. On May Day in England, a local man was encased in a tall wicker framework that was covered with holly and ivy.

4. This figure was followed by chimney sweeps, who collected money from onlookers.

5. This green man, who was called Jack-in-the-Green, represented the reviving life of plants and trees.

6. In parts of Russia and the Balkans, the equivalent of Jack-in-the-Green was Green George, who masqueraded as a tree.

7. On April 23, which is Saint George's Day, the villagers felled a tree, decorated it, and carried it in a procession.

8. Green George was often dunked in a stream to ensure rain, which was needed to keep the fields green.

9. Evergreen plants, which stay green all winter, inspired the Christian symbol of hope for eternal life.

10. In popular Islamic belief, the green one is Khidr, who long ago dived through the spring of life.

EXERCISE B   Underline each adjective clause in the following sentences. Then, draw an arrow to the word modified by each adjective clause.

> **EXAMPLE 1.** The next book you should read is Amy Tan's *The Joy Luck Club*.

1. The subjects we are studying include the history of Venezuela and the geography of Brazil.

2. It was one of those perfect June days poets write about.

3. Leshia operates a small farm she inherited from her grandfather.

4. We enjoy luxuries kings and queens could not have imagined in the old days.

5. Language is the most important tool human beings have developed.

| WORSHEET 3 | Identifying and Using Noun Clauses (Rule 7 e) |

EXERCISE A   Underline each noun clause. Then, on the line provided, indicate how each noun clause is used by writing *S* for subject, *DO* for direct object, *IO* for indirect object, *PN* for predicate nominative, or *OP* for object of a preposition.

EXAMPLE ___DO___ **1.** Did you know <u>that the Egyptian pyramids are all that remain of the Seven Wonders of the Ancient World</u>?

_____ **1.** The public pays little attention to who produces a movie.

_____ **2.** Send whoever requests a subscription a newsletter.

_____ **3.** One tourist asked who is buried in the Taj Mahal.

_____ **4.** Esperanza's excuse was that she had lost my address.

_____ **5.** An inland sea once covered most of what is now the state of Utah.

_____ **6.** Whether or not other galaxies might be inhabited is an interesting problem.

_____ **7.** Shibasaburo Kitasato's discovery was that bubonic plague is carried by rat fleas.

_____ **8.** Drivers should realize that cars can be as deadly as guns.

_____ **9.** Do you know who identified radium as an element?

_____ **10.** What caused the craters on the moon is being investigated.

EXERCISE B   To each of the following groups of words, add a noun clause to make a complete sentence. The use of each noun clause is given in parentheses.

EXAMPLE **1.** (*subject*) is surprising news. *That the mayor resigned is surprising news.*

1. The waiter at the Lebanese restaurant offered (*indirect object*) the extra falafels. _____

2. Just serve me a little of (*object of preposition*). _____

3. Sean appreciated (*direct object*). _____

4. (*subject*) gave me courage and hope. _____

5. You can pass the ball to (*object of preposition*). _____

Continued ☞

6. A long and heavy rain is (*predicate nominative*). _____

_____

7. Mrs. Murdock praised (*direct object*). _____

_____

8. (*subject*) remains your decision. _____

_____

9. The judges will give (*indirect object*) the prize. _____

_____

10. Do you know (*direct object*)? _____

_____

11. The insufficient funds were no surprise to (*object of preposition*). _____

_____

12. Do the records indicate (*direct object*)? _____

_____

13. Tomorrow, I will bring (*indirect object*) the recipe for my Christmas salad. _____

_____

14. (*subject*) made that particular Ramadan a special time for them. _____

_____

15. Amy didn't know (*direct object*). _____

_____

16. Considering (*object of preposition*), he appeared to be following a plan. _____

_____

17. (*subject*) made me very happy. _____

_____

18. Mr. Dawkins asked (*direct object*). _____

_____

19. The correct answer was (*predicate nominative*). _____

_____

20. Which businesses offer (*indirect object*) on-the-job training? _____

_____

LANGUAGE HANDBOOK 7 CLAUSES

WORKSHEET 4 | **Using Adverb Clauses (Rule 7 f)**

EXERCISE A   Underline each adverb clause in the following sentences.

> **EXAMPLE 1.** I bought J. E. Zimmerman's *Dictionary of Classical Mythology* <u>after I read *D'Aulaires' Book of Greek Myths*.</u>

1. If you read Greek mythology, you can discover many interesting stories.

2. Until I read the story of the Amazons, I had not heard of this race of fighting women.

3. Several Greek heroes tried to subdue the Amazons because these women wished to live independently of Greek society.

4. In one story Heracles conquered them when he obtained the belt of their queen.

5. In another story, Theseus of Athens conquered the Amazons as if the conquest of Heracles had never taken place.

6. After the Amazons were defeated, Theseus married one of them.

7. Although the Amazons married men from another region, they kept only their female children.

8. If an Amazon had a male child, she gave him to the father to raise.

9. Since the battles between the Greek heroes and these women warriors were so dramatic, they are often depicted in works of art.

10. When I view reproductions of Greek vases, I look for representations of the battles with the Amazons.

EXERCISE B   Convert each compound sentence to a complex sentence by changing the italicized independent clause to an adverb clause. Be sure to add a comma after any adverb clause that precedes the independent clause.

> **EXAMPLE 1.** *We turned on the faucet*, and no water came out. <u>When we turned on the faucet, no water came out.</u>

1. *The car sped away*, and we took down the license number. _____

_____

2. *The vote was close*, and Mr. Chavez demanded a recount. _____

_____

3. The food is poor, but *it is quite expensive*. _____

_____

4. *You wait long enough*, and everything comes back into style again. _____

_____

5. *Mother loves canaries*, and we gave her one for her birthday. _____

_____

Continued ☞

6. *The vegetables are fresh*, and they are very good. _____
_____

7. *Our dog hears a siren*, and he hides under the sofa. _____
_____

8. The papers will be returned, and *we can correct them.* _____
_____

9. *Don took a summer writing course*, and his grades improved a great deal. _____
_____

10. *Lu is working as a legal secretary*, and she is studying for the bar exam at night. _____
_____

11. *Phyllis likes swimming*, and her parents gave her a season pass for the local pool. _____
_____

12. Zack's kite soared high into the sky, and *the wind blew enough to push it along.* _____
_____

13. Sharon is riding to work with us, and *the mechanic can get her car repaired.* _____
_____

14. *My grandparents have wanted to take this trip for a long time*, and they are excited. _____
_____
_____

15. *We can meet our deadlines,* and we will be adding two more shifts. _____
_____

16. We want to take our dog along, and *we are going on our vacation.* _____
_____

17. Arthur checked the oncoming traffic, and *he entered the freeway.* _____
_____

18. *William was here this morning,* and did you see him? _____
_____
_____

19. I don't mind putting those covers on my books, and *each one is a different color.* _____
_____
_____

20. *More parking spaces were added this year,* and our school parking lot is still crowded.
_____
_____

LANGUAGE
HANDBOOK **7** CLAUSES

WORSHEET 5 | **Using Adverb Clauses and Elliptical Clauses (Rules 7 f, g)**

EXERCISE A   In each of the following word groups, you will find two italicized subordinating conjunctions. After each subordinating conjunction, fill in the blank to make an adverb clause that will make sense in relation to the independent clause already given.

EXAMPLE **1.** *If* _____*you have a radio*_____ , you can get news
wherever _____*you happen to live*_____ .

1. *Unless* _____, you won't find it *when* _____.

2. You will do a better job *if* _____ *before* _____.

3. *Although* _____, I finished "The Weary Blues" *before* _____.

4. I opened a bank account *so that* _____ *when* _____.

5. *Since* _____, I always pay attention *while* _____.

EXERCISE B   In each of the following sentences, underline the elliptical clause and supply the missing words that will complete the clause's meaning.

EXAMPLE **1.** Akosua knows that Brenda likes art <u>as much as she.</u> *does* _____

1. Julian has read more of Gary Soto's writing than I. _____

_____

2. When climbing a mountain, be sure to wear proper footwear. _____

_____

3. I take the trash out more often than they. _____

_____

4. While writing his report, Elias learned about the history of the Choctaw. _____

_____

5. The sisters frequently fought when teenagers. _____

_____

6. I've tried, but I can't make corn pudding as well as she. _____

_____

7. While at summer camp, the boys swam one hundred laps every day. _____

_____

8. Janet conjugated the French verbs faster than Kate. _____

_____

9. Most people require solitude when writing poetry. _____

_____

Continued ☞

10. The scientists performed the experiment as before. _____

_____

11. Although cold and wet, she continued to look for the lost dog. _____

_____

12. When finished staining the deck, be sure to clean the paintbrushes. _____

_____

13. While working as a baby sitter, Brianna learned to be very patient. _____

_____

14. Once ready, we can leave. _____

_____

15. Do you think Karen has worked longer than Dan? _____

_____

16. The telephone seems to have rung more today than yesterday. _____

_____

17. While exciting, the special effects are not as good as those in the other movie. _____

_____

18. When dreaming, I often think I'm flying. _____

_____

19. Florida has a longer coastline than Louisiana. _____

_____

20. Do you think this computer manual is easier to read than that one? _____

_____

21. Despite years of lessons, I can't sing as well as he. _____

_____

22. When giving babies a bath, never leave them alone in the tub. _____

_____

23. Although pressed for time, my math teacher explained the theorem again. _____

_____

24. Does Saturday night's concert cost more than this one? _____

_____

25. This bowl of quéso is spicier than the other one. _____

_____

LANGUAGE HANDBOOK 7 CLAUSES

WORSHEET 6 Test (Rules 7 a–g)

EXERCISE A   To each of the following groups of words, add an independent clause or a subordinate clause as indicated in parentheses.

> **EXAMPLE** **1.** (*independent clause*) after the movie ended. _The audience was_
> _totally silent after the movie ended._

1. It was my father (*subordinate clause*). _____

_____

2. If I ruled the world (*independent clause*). _____

_____

3. Kwan lived in New York's Chinatown (*subordinate clause*). _____

_____

_____

4. When we go camping (*independent clause*). _____

_____

_____

5. (*subordinate clause*) I'd buy a car of my own. _____

_____

_____

6. They told the candidates (*subordinate clause*). _____

_____

_____

7. Here is my program from the performance of *Porgy and Bess* (*subordinate clause*). _____

_____

_____

8. Where are the Chihuahuas (*subordinate clause*)? _____

_____

_____

9. (*independent clause*) when I learned how to read. _____

_____

_____

10. I won't have much spare time (*subordinate clause*). _____

_____

_____

Continued ☞

LANGUAGE HANDBOOK 7 **WORKSHEET 6** *(continued)*

EXERCISE B To each of the following groups of words, add a clause to complete the sentence. The type of each clause is given in parentheses.

EXAMPLE 1. It was probably the potatoes (*adjective clause*). _It was probably_
the potatoes that made me thirsty.

1. Rosamond takes her Australian shepherd (*adverb clause*). _____

_____

2. Phillipe went to the recycling center to take the bottles (*adjective clause*). _____

_____

3. (*elliptical clause*) the Marshalls ran into old friends. _____

_____

4. As science students, do you know (*noun clause*). _____

_____

5. The Brazilian dancers felt (*adverb clause*). _____

_____

6. Japanese American art is (*noun clause*). _____

_____

7. Edgar Allan Poe is a poet (*adjective clause*). _____

_____

8. (*noun clause*) can influence your life tomorrow. _____

_____

9. We'll stop at the store (*adjective clause*). _____

_____

10. (*adverb clause*) they should be here by today. _____

_____

11. The principal's message was (*noun clause*). _____

_____

12. I live near the airport (*adjective clause*). _____

_____

13. This band has a better vocalist (*adverb clause*). _____

_____

14. Do you understand (*noun clause*)? _____

_____

Continued ☞

15. (*elliptical clause*) the airplane continued to fly. _____

_____

16. The weathered log cabin, (*adjective clause*), had stood for two hundred years. _____

_____

17. (*adverb clause*), you will find friendly people. _____

_____

18. The millionaire would leave his money to (*noun clause*). _____

_____

19. The campground (*adjective clause*) has a beautiful lake. _____

_____

20. We know that the politician is (*noun clause*). _____

_____

EXERCISE C   Underline the subordinate clause in each sentence. Then, label each subordinate clause by writing *ADV* for adverb, *ADJ* for adjective, or *N* for noun.

> EXAMPLE _____N_____ **1.** In 1995, University of South Carolina archaeologists discovered <u>what they believed to be the wreck of the *H. L. Hunley*</u>.

_____ **1.** The first submarine that ever sank a warship was designed for the Confederacy by Horace L. Hunley.

_____ **2.** It could reach a speed of four miles per hour if the wind and the tide were right.

_____ **3.** The crew propelled the small ship, which was built from a converted boiler, by turning several hand cranks.

_____ **4.** Although it cruised only three inches below the surface, it could submerge to a depth of six feet.

_____ **5.** Its only victim was the Federal sloop *Housatonic*, which it sank off Charleston on February 17, 1864.

_____ **6.** One night a lookout on the *Housatonic* reported that a planklike object was approaching the ship.

_____ **7.** He couldn't imagine what the strange object might be.

_____ **8.** In the violent explosion which soon followed, the *Housatonic* went to the bottom; the submarine sank soon afterward.

_____ **9.** Before it met its final fate, the *H. L. Hunley* had been sunk three times and had drowned more than twenty men, including its inventor.

_____ **10.** Naval experts say that the *Hunley* was the grandparent of the modern submarine.

LANGUAGE HANDBOOK **8** SENTENCE STRUCTURE

WORKSHEET 1 Identifying Sentences (Rule 8 a)

EXERCISE A   On the line provided, identify each of the following groups of words as sentence fragments (*F*) or complete sentences (*S*).

EXAMPLES ___*F*___ **1.** Runs sixty miles per hour.

___*S*___ **2.** We listened to the gentle patter of the rain on the roof.

_____ **1.** Eleven elephants stomped across the field.

_____ **2.** Listens carefully to the instructions.

_____ **3.** Eudora about Sojourner Truth.

_____ **4.** Blind dates can be nerve-racking for both people.

_____ **5.** What is your favorite kind of food?

_____ **6.** A nice change of pace for the family.

_____ **7.** Participated in the annual powwow.

_____ **8.** The mall will open at 10:00 A.M. Saturday.

_____ **9.** Talking on the phone intimidates Gavin.

_____ **10.** Two cranes the enormous roof beams.

EXERCISE B   Decide whether the following items are sentences or fragments. If an item is already a complete sentence, write *C* on the line provided. If the item is a fragment, rewrite the item as a complete sentence.

EXAMPLE **1.** Decided to buy a class ring. *Carla decided to buy a class ring.*

1. Mrs. Warren to the state convention. _____

_____

2. Wants to work for world peace. _____

_____

3. Diane lives on a remote ranch in central Oregon. _____

_____

4. Wrote a fascinating report about the Kiowa calendar. _____

_____

5. Having to do with new audio systems. _____

_____

Continued ☞

6. Usually runs later than the scheduled time. _____

_____

7. Have you seen many early films from India? _____

_____

8. The restaurant's live music on Saturday nights. _____

_____

9. A day in the life of a salamander. _____

_____

10. You may borrow my calculator if you need to figure your taxes. _____

_____

EXERCISE C   Each item below consists of two word groups. If they are both complete sentences, insert a period following the first sentence and correctly capitalize the first word of the second sentence. If the two word groups form one complete sentence, write *C* on the line provided.

EXAMPLES _____ **1.** I am learning to play chess. *I*t requires much concentration.

_____*C*_____ **2.** The novel has one of those plots   that keep you guessing.

_____ **1.** Yetta practiced every day   because she wanted to be a famous violinist.

_____ **2.** We're going to read *Moby-Dick*   it's a novel about the great white whale.

_____ **3.** We all timed ourselves   to see if we could improve our speed.

_____ **4.** Out of the water climbed Mike   who had fallen overboard.

_____ **5.** Cardinals are especially welcome in winter   they look pretty against the snow.

_____ **6.** There will be a lecture by Reginald McKnight   he will speak about writing fiction.

_____ **7.** The thesaurus came from her aunt   who is a practicing attorney.

_____ **8.** All of us were sorry   to have missed seeing the eclipse.

_____ **9.** In their Ohio travels   European settlers found many American Indian burial mounds.

_____ **10.** The wind swirled across the snow   the gusts blew it into drifts.

LANGUAGE HANDBOOK 8 SENTENCE STRUCTURE

WORKSHEET 2 **Identifying Subject and Predicate (Rules 8 b–g)**

EXERCISE   First, use a vertical line or lines to separate the complete subject from the complete predicate. Then, draw one line under the simple subject and two lines under the verb. Be sure to include all words in a verb phrase and all parts of a compound subject or compound verb.

> **EXAMPLES** **1.** The clever <u>magician</u>|<u><u>performed</u></u> two tricks for us.
>
> **2.** The <u>car</u>|<u><u>has</u></u> room for five adults and <u><u>saves</u></u> gasoline.
>
> **3.** During class today,|<u>each</u> of you|<u><u>will begin</u></u> the outline for your paper.

1. The nation of Indonesia has the world's second longest coastline.

2. In the White Mountains, the bristlecone pine tree grows.

3. Some of the trees were already ancient two thousand years ago.

4. Sequoias and redwoods also live for many years.

5. Many animals in the desert hide underground by day and hunt at night.

6. The shark swims very swiftly and hunts ruthlessly.

7. Many people have enjoyed camping and hiking.

8. Volunteer work at the hospital benefits the community and teaches many skills to the volunteer.

9. Both running and walking are good exercise for young and old alike.

10. We learn anatomy and first aid in this class.

11. The Cambodian alphabet contains seventy-four letters.

12. In Missouri in 1812, a strong earthquake occurred.

13. The popularity of soccer in the United States has grown rapidly.

14. We read about life in a Welsh mining town in *How Green Was My Valley*.

15. Most astronomers subscribe to the big-bang theory.

16. Beans and eggs are rich in protein.

17. Our neighbors came from Mexico and visit there every year.

18. Where are the steps leading to the second floor?

19. Either chemistry or biology fulfills your science requirement.

20. The first effective treatment for malaria was developed by Peruvian Indians.

21. Here is my English composition.

22. The coach and the referee disagreed about the play.

23. The head of the committee has asked for everyone's help.

24. A wild duck circled above the pond and flew away over the treetops.

25. The Festival of the Kitchen God is held before the Chinese New Year.

| WORKSHEET 3 | **Identifying and Using Compound Subjects and Compound Verbs (Rules 8 e, f)** |

EXERCISE A   Underline the compound subjects and verbs in each of the following sentences. Then, on the line provided, write *CS* for compound subject or *CV* for compound verb.

EXAMPLE ____*CV*____ **1.** The appaloosas <u>ate</u> alfalfa and <u>drank</u> water at the corral.

_____ **1.** Corn, squash, and berries were cultivated by southeastern American Indians.

_____ **2.** The two cats fight and play together.

_____ **3.** Aleta, Keo, and Leroy are making fresh fruit salads.

_____ **4.** Gabriel steeped and boiled the purple potion.

_____ **5.** Will you wash, iron, and fold the clothes for me?

_____ **6.** Forty-six alligators lurk and swim in the ponds on the university campus.

_____ **7.** The Olmec, Maya, Aztec, and Inca developed very advanced civilizations.

_____ **8.** Tomorrow and the day after are the days for cross-country events.

_____ **9.** The writer Edgar Lee Masters grew up in Illinois, but was born in Kansas.

_____ **10.** Poor working conditions and the lack of overtime pay were reasons for the strike.

_____ **11.** How many police cars, ambulances, and trucks were included in the drill?

_____ **12.** For two months, our friends and neighbors have been planning our block party.

_____ **13.** Edward had bought fence slats and had loaded them into his truck.

_____ **14.** Would you stop and look at the size of those trees!

_____ **15.** Jan and Denise will be loaning me their notes to study for the math test.

_____ **16.** Should Fran wash and dry these clothes now or later?

_____ **17.** Perhaps we will find the solution and win the game.

_____ **18.** Late today, the ambassador and his assistants left for meetings in Paris.

_____ **19.** When did the librarian see these books and check them out to you?

_____ **20.** This year, Bo and Jeepers should have won the amazing pet contest.

EXERCISE B   Combine each set of sentences to create one sentence with a compound subject or a compound verb. Write the new sentence on the line provided.

EXAMPLE **1.** The boxes are packed. The suitcases are also packed. *The boxes and suitcases are packed.*

1. The full moon makes Fang bark. Of course, any light makes Fang bark. _____

_____

Continued ☞

2. Sasha walks on beaches. She looks for seashells. She also builds sandcastles. _____

_____

_____

3. The volleyball needs to be put in the car. The net and picnic basket also need to be put in the car. _____

_____

_____

4. The tortillas are for supper. The guacamole and grated cheese are also for supper. _____

_____

_____

5. Mamud writes for the newspaper. He sometimes copyedits it, too. _____

_____

_____

6. In 1954, the U.S. Supreme Court declared segregated schools to be illegal. The court also ordered states to integrate their schools speedily. _____

_____

_____

7. Jaguars are exotic wild cats. Cheetahs are also exotic wild cats. _____

_____

_____

8. Chemistry interests me as a career. Physics also interests me. Botany would make an interesting career, too. _____

_____

_____

9. Aunt Flossie raises Australian shepherds. She often wins blue ribbons with them at dog shows.

_____

_____

10. Venice, Italy, is a beautiful city built on islands. Stockholm, Sweden, is a beautiful city built on islands. _____

_____

_____

Elements of Literature

LANGUAGE HANDBOOK **8** **SENTENCE STRUCTURE**

| WORKSHEET 4 | **Finding the Subject in Different Types of Sentences (Rule 8 g)**

EXERCISE   First, underline the verb in each of the following sentences. Be sure to include any helping verbs. Then, locate the subject by asking *Who?* or *What?* before the verb and circle the subject. In sentences that give orders or make requests, underline the verb and write the understood subject *you* in parentheses after the sentence.

EXAMPLES 1. In 1969, (Golda Meir) became prime minister of Israel.

2. Take these clothes to the dry cleaner before 6:00 P.M. today. ((you))

1. Have you ever eaten hummus?

2. Please reply to this request before October 1.

3. Up and up went the hot-air balloon.

4. There are 220 yards in a furlong.

5. Did Buddhism originate in India?

6. Take your soccer ball outside!

7. In the distance whirled the funnel of the tornado.

8. Here is my history paper on the League of Nations.

9. Do you like science fiction by Isaac Asimov?

10. Come over here with those groceries, please.

11. Not one shooting star have I ever seen.

12. There was no list of answers in the back of the book.

13. Up the path came Jorge, with a string of fish in his hand.

14. Do not be late to class any more.

15. Why did Mrs. Kitazato decide to cut her hair?

16. Fold the application on the dotted line.

17. Here are the inventory sheets for the school store.

18. Such an adorable puppy will soon find a new home.

19. There is a sale on porch furniture at Silverman's.

20. Where is the chuck key for this electric drill?

21. On our street lives a Thai family.

22. Just ask me anything about country music.

23. There is a need in the band for an oboe player.

24. Is Quito the capital of Ecuador?

25. There, on the ground, lay my class ring.

LANGUAGE HANDBOOK 8 SENTENCE STRUCTURE

WORKSHEET 5 | Identifying Complements (Rules 8 h–l)

EXERCISE In the following sentences, identify how each italicized complement is used by writing *PA* for predicate adjective, *PN* for predicate nominative, *DO* for direct object, *IO* for indirect object, or *OC* for objective complement.

EXAMPLE ___DO___ **1.** Margaret Fuller began her *career* as a teacher.

_____ **1.** Many people considered her a *woman* of extraordinary intellect and energy.

_____ **2.** Born in 1810, she was reading *Latin* at the age of eight.

_____ **3.** John Quincy Adams attended her formal *debut* into Boston society in 1826.

_____ **4.** Her parents gave *society* a thinker rather than a social butterfly.

_____ **5.** She became a *member* of a literary circle including Ralph Waldo Emerson and Henry David Thoreau.

_____ **6.** These transcendentalist writers began their own quarterly *magazine*.

_____ **7.** They made her *editor* of the quarterly.

_____ **8.** Eventually, The Dial became a *focus* for an emerging American literature.

_____ **9.** The publication was *one* of the most important periodicals in American literary history.

_____ **10.** She also taught *children* foreign languages.

_____ **11.** In 1845 she earned *herself* an international reputation as an advocate of women's rights.

_____ **12.** Her book Woman in the Nineteenth Century was *revolutionary* in its day.

_____ **13.** The book criticized economic, social, and political *discrimination* against women.

_____ **14.** Today its arguments sound *familiar*.

_____ **15.** Margaret Fuller also became a newspaper *reporter*.

_____ **16.** Horace Greeley of the New York Tribune was her *employer*.

_____ **17.** At first she wrote literary *reviews* for the Tribune.

_____ **18.** Later she championed social *reforms* such as the abolition of capital punishment and better treatment for the mentally ill.

_____ **19.** Margaret Fuller spent her last *years* in Italy as a foreign correspondent and as a sympathizer with the Italian republican cause.

_____ **20.** Her death was *untimely*; she drowned at sea in 1850.

Elements of Literature

LANGUAGE HANDBOOK **8** **SENTENCE STRUCTURE**

WORSHEET 6 | **Identifying Direct Objects and Indirect Objects (Rules 8 i–k)**

EXERCISE A   On the line provided, identify the underlined words in the following sentences as direct objects (*DO*) or indirect objects (*IO*).

         EXAMPLE   __*IO*__   **1.** The French Club gave <u>her</u> a certificate of appreciation.

_____   **1.** In the 1920s, Zora Neale Hurston wrote <u>stories and plays</u> about the African American experience.

_____   **2.** Her successful musical reviews portrayed black folk <u>culture</u>.

_____   **3.** Hurston's stories gave other <u>people</u> exposure to the oral tales she heard.

_____   **4.** In 1937, Hurston published *Their Eyes Were Watching God*, considered to be her best novel.

_____   **5.** Contemporary African American writers owe <u>Hurston</u> a great deal for being a forerunner.

_____   **6.** Our literature class discussed our favorite <u>authors</u>.

_____   **7.** Mr. Chan told <u>us</u> that his favorite is Jack London.

_____   **8.** Other people's choices ran the <u>gamut</u> from Stephen King to Shakespeare.

_____   **9.** We chose reading <u>partners</u> and traded favorite books.

_____   **10.** My partner, Anne, gave <u>me</u> *Les Misérables* to read.

EXERCISE B   Underline the objective complements in the following sentences.

         EXAMPLE **1.** The panel considered Celia Trevino <u>the most qualified applicant</u>.

1. They made the old house a showplace.

2. The team appointed Jeff captain.

3. Her friends call Reiko compassionate and generous.

4. My friends and I call movies our greatest entertainment.

5. The children finger-painted the walls bright pink and yellow.

EXERCISE C   In the following sentences, underline direct objects once and indirect objects twice. Circle objective complements.

         EXAMPLE **1.** Sandra considers the <u>dog</u> a ⟨menace⟩.

1. Dylan's uncle sent him an invitation to a camping trip in the mountains.

2. Hafez served us tabbouleh and pita bread.

3. The storms swept the yard clean.

4. Bianca appointed her daughter family historian.

5. They call the hamsters Serenity and Playful.

LANGUAGE
HANDBOOK **8** SENTENCE STRUCTURE

WORSHEET 7 | **Identifying and Using Predicate Nominatives and Predicate Adjectives (Rule 8 l)**

EXERCISE A   In the following sentences, underline the predicate nominative or predicate adjective once and the linking verb twice. On the line provided, indicate whether the complement is a predicate nominative (*PN*) or a predicate adjective (*PA*).

EXAMPLE ___PN___ **1.** My favorite sport is spelunking.

_____ **1.** After months of neglect, the once tame cat became a feral animal.

_____ **2.** The huevos rancheros and roasted potatoes tasted delicious.

_____ **3.** Garrett Hongo's poetry is beautiful to read aloud.

_____ **4.** The winners of the trivia quiz are Araba, Charlotte, and Amadeo.

_____ **5.** After the dry spell the rain feels marvelous.

_____ **6.** The symphonic band's concert was inspiring.

_____ **7.** Some books, like the Bible, remain bestsellers forever.

_____ **8.** Who said, "Nothing is certain except death and taxes"?

_____ **9.** Brianna's favorite book is Walt Whitman's *Leaves of Grass*.

_____ **10.** The little black bear was afraid.

EXERCISE B   On the line provided, add a predicate nominative or predicate adjective to each group of words below to make a complete sentence.

EXAMPLE **1.** The bells in the chapel sound *The bells in the chapel sound*
melodious.

1. The train should be _____

_____

2. My pet llama is _____

_____

3. Since Bernard's induction into the hall of fame, he seems _____

_____

4. All of the vegetables and flowers they planted grew _____

_____

5. Contemporary poetry and fiction can be _____

_____

Continued ☞

6. The tired circus animals grew _____

_____

7. The decorations for the Cinco de Mayo party were _____

_____

8. Minna Lea, at age seventy, became _____

_____

9. The pasta and breadsticks smell _____

_____

10. All of the sports events will be _____

_____

11. Among the supplies we found in the cabinet were _____

_____

12. Cheryl's favorite colors are _____

_____

13. By afternoon, the sky had turned _____

_____

14. Todd still remains _____

_____

15. This time next month, we will be _____

_____

16. The magician's beard became _____

_____

17. Only the ripest grapes were _____

_____

18. The bugle call sounded _____

_____

19. Plants in the garden appear _____

_____

20. Fresh-baked bread had always been _____

_____

LANGUAGE HANDBOOK 8 SENTENCE STRUCTURE

WORKSHEET 8 Classifying Sentences According to Structure (Rule 8 m)

EXERCISE A On the line provided, classify each of the following sentences as simple (*S*), compound (*CD*), complex (*CX*), or compound-complex (*CD-CX*).

EXAMPLE ___CD___ **1.** They read the instructions aloud, and Ana put together the model plane.

_____ **1.** Would you please water the rosebushes and the crape myrtle?

_____ **2.** After the paint dried, Dominic made a frame for the painting.

_____ **3.** We had an hour for the test; however, when the timer went off, Ms. Feynman gave us another ten minutes.

_____ **4.** Pythons are some of the world's largest snakes.

_____ **5.** Like other large snakes, pythons eat small animals; furthermore, pythons may also hunt prey as large as wild pigs.

_____ **6.** Barika used a camera loaded with high-speed film and fitted with a telephoto lens to take pictures of hummingbirds.

_____ **7.** *Native Son*, which is Richard Wright's first book, brought him recognition as a writer.

_____ **8.** Seattle and Spokane are at opposite ends of Washington; moreover, the Cascade Range of mountains lies between them.

_____ **9.** The names of both cities come from American Indian words.

_____ **10.** The term *pagoda* refers to the style of building that is used for Buddhist houses of worship in China, Japan, and other countries, but the word came from India.

EXERCISE B On the lines provided, use the groups of words given to create the kind of sentence indicated in parentheses.

EXAMPLE **1.** The dogs run to meet me (*complex*) *The dogs run to meet me* *when I get home from school.*

1. After the race started (*complex*) _____

_____

2. As far as I am concerned, the ideal pet would be (*compound-complex*) _____

_____

3. The object of recycling is (*simple*) _____

_____

4. The most interesting historical events (*compound*) _____

_____

Continued ☞

5. They planned to enter the contest (*compound-complex*) _____
_____

6. The skunk in the road (*complex*) _____
_____

7. When the alarm went off (*compound-complex*) _____
_____

8. The cars at the rally (*simple*) _____
_____

9. Collecting old books is (*compound*) _____
_____

10. There was nothing in the refrigerator (*complex*) _____
_____

11. The blacksmith's anvil sat (*simple*) _____
_____

12. Wherever Alicia and Joel went on their vacation (*complex*) _____
_____

13. Long lines snaked through the parking lot (*compound*) _____
_____

14. Once we knew in which direction we wanted to go (*compound-complex*) _____
_____

15. Several of our friends were running for class offices (*compound*) _____
_____

16. No one had the slightest idea (*complex*) _____
_____

17. Barbara left the boat (*complex*) _____
_____

18. Racing to the finish line was (*simple*) _____
_____

19. Our class was still having trouble with the chemistry equation (*compound*) _____
_____

20. Before we left (*compound-complex*) _____
_____

LANGUAGE HANDBOOK **8** SENTENCE STRUCTURE

| WORKSHEET 9 | **Classifying Sentences According to Purpose (Rule 8 n)** |

EXERCISE A   On the line provided, identify each of the following sentences as *DEC* for declarative, *INT* for interrogative, *IMP* for imperative, or *EXC* for exclamatory. Then, supply the appropriate end mark after the last word in each sentence.

EXAMPLE _____*INT*_____ **1.** Will you please find this address on the map**?**

_____ **1.** Wow, what a beautiful sunset

_____ **2.** Have you read Stevie Smith's poetry

_____ **3.** Hand me that pair of pliers

_____ **4.** Water birds, such as ducks, have naturally waterproof feathers

_____ **5.** When do you expect to be through repairing the brakes on the car

_____ **6.** We are doing Dr. Martin Luther King, Jr.'s "Letter from Birmingham City Jail" as a choral reading.

_____ **7.** Don't look down

_____ **8.** Be sure to keep fresh batteries in your smoke detectors

_____ **9.** Why don't oil and water mix

_____ **10.** Time and tide wait for no one

EXERCISE B   On the lines provided, write the sort of sentence indicated in parentheses, using the verb provided.

EXAMPLE **1.** write (*interrogative sentence*) *Can you write your research report in one week?*

1. scare (*declarative sentence*) _____

_____

2. scare (*imperative sentence*) _____

_____

3. scare (*interrogative sentence*) _____

_____

4. scare (*exclamatory sentence*) _____

_____

5. work (*declarative sentence*) _____

_____

Continued ☞

6. work (*imperative sentence*) _____

_____

7. work (*interrogative sentence*) _____

_____

8. work (*exclamatory sentence*) _____

_____

9. talk (*interrogative sentence*) _____

_____

10. talk (*imperative sentence*) _____

_____

11. talk (*exclamatory sentence*) _____

_____

12. talk (*declarative sentence*) _____

_____

13. claim (*declarative sentence*) _____

_____

14. claim (*imperative sentence*) _____

_____

15. claim (*exclamatory sentence*) _____

_____

16. claim (*interrogative sentence*) _____

_____

17. growl (*declarative sentence*) _____

_____

18. growl (*imperative sentence*) _____

_____

19. growl (*exclamatory sentence*) _____

_____

20. growl (*interrogative sentence*) _____

_____

LANGUAGE HANDBOOK 8 SENTENCE STRUCTURE

WORKSHEET 10 Test (Rules 8 a–n)

EXERCISE A On the lines provided, identify each of the following groups of words as a sentence (*S*) or a fragment (*F*).

EXAMPLE ____F____ **1.** If the moon rises at seven tonight.

_____ **1.** Have you read Maxine Hong Kingston's book, *The Woman Warrior?*

_____ **2.** Fields of grains and vegetables.

_____ **3.** A spider's web is designed to capture and hold insects.

_____ **4.** Some time before the paint is dry.

_____ **5.** Explodes on contact.

EXERCISE B For each independent clause in the following sentences, underline the simple subject once and the simple predicate twice. If the subject is the understood subject *you,* write *you* in parentheses after the sentence and underline it once. Be sure to include all parts of a compound subject or compound verb. On the line provided, identify the purpose of each sentence as declarative (*DEC*), imperative (*IMP*), interrogative (*INT*), or exclamatory (*EXC*). Add the correct end punctuation. Then, on the same line, classify each sentence according to structure as simple (*S*), compound (*CD*), complex (*CX*), or compound-complex (*CD-CX*). Do not confuse compound subjects and verbs with compound sentences.

EXAMPLES ___DEC, CX___ **1.** The <u>lions</u> and <u>tigers</u> at Turpentine Creek <u>have been rescued</u> from owners who neglected them.

___IMP, S___ **2.** <u>Stop</u> the car! (<u>you</u>)

_____ **1.** Igneous rocks are volcanic; in other words, they were once molten

_____ **2.** Do you know what makes the properties of igneous rocks different

_____ **3.** The size of the crystals in the rocks is determined by the rate of cooling

_____ **4.** Lava that cools quickly forms very small crystals, but lava that cools slowly forms large crystals

_____ **5.** Obsidian, an igneous rock that cools quickly enough to form very small or no crystals, has been used around the world for centuries

_____ **6.** In many countries, people still use it for jewelry

_____ **7.** What a beautiful stone it is

_____ **8.** Can you believe that pumice, an igneous rock formed from lava, is lightweight enough to float on water

_____ **9.** American Indians used flint, which is a sedimentary rock, for spear and arrow points

_____ **10.** Don't handle flint carelessly

WORKSHEET 1 | Coordinating Ideas (Rule 9 a)

EXERCISE Each item below consists of two separate clauses. If the clauses are *related* and *of equal importance*, combine them into a compound sentence. If the clauses are not closely related, make them into two separate sentences by supplying an end mark and a capital letter.

EXAMPLES **1.** Our town is small   it is growing rapidly. _Our town is small, but it is growing rapidly._

2. Our town is small   it is growing rapidly. _Our town is small; however, it is growing rapidly._

3. Keith is in my civics class   his sister is a reporter. _Keith is in my civics class. His sister is a reporter._

1. The nights were clear   the sky was full of stars. _____

_____

2. Doctor Siddiqui is quite young   she is a graduate of Ohio State. _____

_____

3. Doctor Siddiqui is quite young   she seems very competent. _____

_____

4. This organic spray kills insects   one of our neighbors uses it. _____

_____

5. My mom just painted our house   we are planning to sell it. _____

_____

6. The parking lot was closed   the attendant had gone home. _____

_____

7. Mrs. Ames is seventy years old   she jogs every day. _____

_____

8. Kip lettered in three sports   he wants to become an artist. _____

_____

9. A product must be advertised   people will not ask for it. _____

_____

10. The book was written by Gloria Naylor   the class enjoyed the book review. _____

_____

_____

Continued ☞

11. Rita recently moved here   she has few friends. _____
_____

12. The program bored the adults   the children enjoyed it. _____
_____

13. My father drove most of the way   we had two flat tires. _____
_____

14. The salesclerk has another new car   she gets them at a discount. _____
_____

15. It hasn't rained for weeks   most of the lawns are brown. _____
_____

16. A large crowd attended the game   the weather was very chilly. _____
_____

17. Vertical stripes make a person look slender   horizontal stripes emphasize stoutness. _____
_____

18. Mr. Freed is a barber   his son won the state piano contest. _____
_____

19. The Cancún sunrises are magnificent   few vacationers ever rise early enough to see them.
_____

20. Diamonds are used to cut steel   they are weighed by the carat. _____
_____

21. The crew worked all day   they were repairing potholes in our street. _____
_____

22. Earthworms can be a great help in a garden   they help to put oxygen in the soil. _____
_____

23. Vegetable prices have risen this year   they will rise next year also. _____
_____

24. Wendy planned to read her notes one more time   she studied for an extra hour. _____
_____

25. Brian and Helen brought paper plates   Jessie, Carla, and I brought the food. _____
_____

LANGUAGE HANDBOOK 9 SENTENCE STYLE

| WORKSHEET 2 | **Subordinating Ideas (Rule 9 b)** |

EXERCISE A   Eliminate the *and*'s in the following sentences by changing the italicized idea to either an adverb or an adjective clause, as the meaning requires. Don't forget to add a comma after an adverb clause at the beginning of a sentence.

EXAMPLE **1.** I think of F. Scott Fitzgerald, and *I think of the Roaring Twenties.*
<u>*Whenever I think of the Roaring Twenties, I think of F. Scott Fitzgerald.*</u>

1. Lupe's room was full of books, and *they showed her interest in science.* _____

_____

_____

2. *The story would have offended many people*, and the paper did not print it. _____

_____

_____

3. Traditional Chinese writing is arranged in vertical columns, and *the columns are read from top to bottom.* _____

_____

_____

4. The mayor made a statement, and *many people disagreed with it.* _____

_____

_____

5. *The auditorium filled up*, and we seated about fifty people on the stage. _____

_____

_____

6. Mom advised Omar to stay near the hotel, and *he would not get lost.* _____

_____

_____

7. This book by Yehuda Amichai was recommended by my friend Angie, and *I value her opinion highly.* _____

_____

_____

8. Zina suggested a plan, and *we all agreed to it.* _____

_____

_____

Continued ☞

LANGUAGE HANDBOOK **9** **WORKSHEET 2** *(continued)*

9. *The <u>Odyssey</u> was written more than 2,500 years ago*, and it is still widely read. _____

_____

_____

10. We visited a farm, and *sheep are raised there for their wool.* _____

_____

_____

EXERCISE B   On the lines provided, rewrite the following sentences to emphasize the idea that is now in the adjective clause and to subordinate the idea that is now in the independent clause. You may have to delete some words, change the word order, or use a different word to begin the new subordinate clause.

EXAMPLE **1.** Sandra Cisneros, who was her parents' only daughter, was born in 1954. *Sandra Cisneros, who was born in 1954, was her parents' only daughter.*

1. Sandra, who had six brothers, often felt excluded from the Cisneros' home life. _____

_____

_____

2. Cisneros, who now realizes the value of that solitude, spent her time reading voraciously.

_____

_____

3. Her experience at the Iowa Writer's Workshop, which earned her a master's degree, encouraged her to find subject matter in her own life. _____

_____

_____

4. Cisneros' first book, which won a prestigious literary award, was *The House on Mango Street.*

_____

_____

5. Cisneros' short stories, poetry, and novels, which weave her unique experience into art, have gained her many readers. _____

_____

_____

6. Euclid, who contributed important work to the field of mathematics, was a Greek of the Hellenistic Age. _____

_____

_____

Continued ☞

7. Geometry, which was developed by Euclid into a system, stems from his discovery of geometric statements of truth. _____

   _____

   _____

8. *Elements*, which was the definitive geometry textbook for a thousand years, was written by Euclid. _____

   _____

   _____

9. Archimedes, who is considered to be the greatest scientist of his age, used mathematics to explain the principle of the lever. _____

   _____

   _____

10. His inventions, which are still in use today, include the block and tackle. _____

    _____

    _____

EXERCISE C For each of the following sentences, write an appropriate subordinating conjunction in the blank. Do not use the same conjunction twice.

   EXAMPLE **1.** _Because_ the car is old, we will not take long trips in it.

1. _____ the rain fell, the desert filled with wildflowers.

2. _____ you finish watching the game, will you have time to repair the toaster?

3. _____ you send the package Priority Mail, it will arrive on time.

4. _____ Amara is building the stone walkway, you could paint the fence.

5. _____ Josh goes, the family dog follows him.

6. _____ the pond will drain correctly, we put a conduit in the levee.

7. _____ someone at the college contacts her, she will apply elsewhere.

8. _____ the piñatas are made, we still need to buy candy to fill them.

9. _____ our homework is completed, we can't go to the concert.

10. _____ we were celebrating Dr. Martin Luther King, Jr.'s birthday, we renamed our stadium for him.

LANGUAGE HANDBOOK 9 SENTENCE STYLE

WORKSHEET 3 | **Using Parallel Structure (Rule 9 c)**

EXERCISE A   Each sentence below contains three ideas that should be expressed with parallel structure. Underline the word group that is not parallel with the others. Then, write the word group correctly on the line provided.

EXAMPLE _to make appointments_ **1.** The duties of the receptionist are to receive visitors, <u>making appointments</u>, and to sort the mail.

_____ **1.** Most of our neighbors are friendly, considerate, and they give help.

_____ **2.** Sales are often held to clear out old stock, for increasing profits, or to advertise the store.

_____ **3.** Del's good grades were due to regular attendance, good participation in class, and he studied effectively.

_____ **4.** Tamisha's report got high marks because of its interesting subject, it covered the topic thoroughly, and it was written on a word processor.

_____ **5.** Before writing your theme, you should prepare a rough outline, collect your material, and a topic should be selected.

_____ **6.** To bake a potato, you should scrub it, pierce it with a fork, and it should be placed on the center rack of the oven.

_____ **7.** We traded in our car because the body was rusty, the worn-out tires, and the engine burned oil.

_____ **8.** Armando finally decided to find a job, to save his earnings, and that he would go to college.

_____ **9.** We made our paper profitable by getting more subscribers, we sold more ads, and by raising its price.

_____ **10.** Science fiction may entertain anyone who has a strong imagination, who is fascinated by the future, and with a yearning for adventure.

EXERCISE B   On the blank line that follows the _and, or, than,_ or _as,_ write the idea printed in parentheses. Make this idea parallel in construction to its partner, which is printed in italics.

EXAMPLE **1.** We enjoyed simple things like _watching the sunrise_ or _walking in the woods_ (a walk in the woods)

1. _A recent book_ is not necessarily better than _____

_____ (one that is old)

2. I often relax _by closing my eyes_ and _____

_____ (picture soft clouds floating in the sky)

3. Our sports editor _attends each game_ and _____

_____ (a report of it is written)

Continued ☞

4. *Seeing other people's faults* is much easier than _____

_____ (to see our own)

5. Exercise *relieves nervous tension* and _____

_____ (the energy level is increased)

6. This test shows *your interests* and _____

_____ (what your abilities are)

7. The committee's chief duties are *to plan programs* and _____

_____ (keeping up the members' interest)

8. Mr. Blumenthal has the habit *of reading the newspaper thoroughly* and _____

_____ (then he forms his opinions)

9. *Hearing Miguel's report on the book* was almost as good as _____

_____ (if I read it myself)

10. Your purpose should be *to discover the truth* rather than _____

_____ (proving yourself right)

11. Our cousins *arrived for a visit* and _____

_____ (are bringing a friend with them)

12. I would rather *ride a bicycle for two miles* than _____

_____ (jogging for one mile)

13. *Listening to your speech* is as good a review of the amendments as _____

_____ (to read the Constitution)

14. Mom expects us *to feed the dog* or _____

_____ (doing some of our other chores)

15. *Finding the epicenter of the earthquake* took longer than _____

_____ (identify its magnitude on the Richter scale)

16. Mr. Owens let us vote on whether we would *hear a guest speaker* or _____

_____ (taking our chemistry test)

17. Gerry preferred *meeting his customers in person* rather than _____

_____ (to talk to them over the phone)

18. Recently, I have had little time *to watch the news* or _____

_____ (reading a book)

19. Parchment was often used *for official documents* and _____

_____ (letters were written on it)

20. At that park, *canoeing* is more popular than _____

_____ (to go swimming)

LANGUAGE
HANDBOOK **9** **SENTENCE STYLE**

| WORSHEET 4 | **Using Parallel Structure (Rule 9 c)**

EXERCISE Revise each of the following sentences to make them parallel.

> **EXAMPLE 1.** Three causes of Hitler's defeat were his failure to invade Britain, he attacked Russia, and the U.S. entrance into the war.
> *Three causes of Hitler's defeat were his failure to invade*
> *Britain, his attack on Russia, and the U.S.'s entrance into the war.*

1. Plants depend upon the soil for anchorage, getting water, and food is absorbed from the soil.

_____

_____

2. Two major functions of cabinet members are to give the president advice and serving as heads of their departments. _____

_____

3. Political parties hold national conventions to draw up a platform, and candidates for the presidency and vice-presidency are selected. _____

_____

4. Three methods of fighting the spread of tuberculosis are to provide free or low-cost screening, treating the disease promptly, and development of better medications. _____

_____

_____

5. The four elements of a plot are exposition, describing complications, the climax, and to resolve the problems. _____

_____

6. Many of Italo Calvino's stories and novels show great imagination, fantastic plots, and are carefully written. _____

_____

7. Jesse increased his silent reading speed by avoiding all lip movement, by taking in several words at one glance, and forced himself to read faster. _____

_____

8. Three objections to business monopolies are that they eliminate competition, limit output, and the fixing of prices. _____

_____

9. Discrimination against women in industry might be eliminated by promotion from within the company, providing training for women employees, and pay equal salaries to men and women doing the same work. _____

_____

10. Mr. Tan maintains the productiveness of his farm's soil by adding compost, certain crops plowed under, and crop rotation. _____

_____

Elements of Literature

LANGUAGE HANDBOOK **9** SENTENCE STYLE

WORKSHEET 5 **Correcting Sentence Fragments (Rule 9 d)**

EXERCISE A   In each of the following items, combine the fragments to make a complete sentence.

> **EXAMPLE 1.** Since early times. People have tried to fly. *People have tried to fly since early times.*

1. Balloons filled with gases lighter than air. People have used since the 1700s. To float above the ground. _____

_____

2. As early as the 1800s. Inventors tried to invent a heavier-than-air machine that would fly. ____

_____

3. Were not meant to carry people. Originally the machines. _____

_____

4. Wilbur and Orville Wright were the first. Flying a powered airplane. In sustained flight. ____

_____

5. The flight lasted 12 seconds. At Kitty Hawk, North Carolina. And went 120 feet. _____

_____

6. They succeeded. They had studied aerodynamics. The principles of the movement of air around objects. _____

_____

7. From this beginning. The airplane industry was started. _____

_____

8. The first pilot to fly across the English Channel. Louis Blériot, a Frenchman. In 1909. _____

_____

_____

Continued ☞

9. The early planes. Were powered by internal combustion engines. Developed by Europeans in the 1800s. _____

_____

_____

10. Later in the twentieth century. Jet engines were developed. Widely used today. _____

_____

_____

EXERCISE B   Some of the following groups of words are complete sentences and some are fragments. If the words form a complete sentence, write *C* on the line provided. If the words form a fragment, revise the fragment on the line provided by supplying or deleting words to make it a complete sentence.

EXAMPLE **1.** Many kinds of bridges in the world. *Many kinds of bridges exist in* *the world.*

1. Arched bridges built on a simple arch, an elongated arch, an arch with a suspended roadway, a bowstring girder beam or tiered arch, or an arch with a supported deck. _____

_____

_____

_____

2. Arched bridges in early times and still in use today. _____

_____

_____

3. Another type of bridge, the cantilever bridge anchored by a supporting structure at one end.

_____

_____

4. Some cantilever bridges are double cantilevers and have supports at both ends. _____

_____

_____

5. The third type of bridge a suspension bridge. _____

_____

_____

6. You may the Golden Gate Bridge in California, which is a suspension bridge. _____

_____

_____

Continued ☞

7. Girder-beam bridges, with crossed pieces, the other type of bridge, often used for railroad trestles. _____

_____

_____

8. Five kinds of girder-beam bridges Warren girder, Pratt truss, Howe truss, Lattice truss, and stayed girder. _____

_____

_____

9. When you look at a bridge now, all the planning that went into it. _____

_____

_____

10. Try to some famous bridges of each type. _____

_____

_____

EXERCISE C The following letter contains some sentence fragments. Rewrite the letter on the lines provided, correcting the sentence fragments by adding or deleting words or combining fragments to make complete sentences.

EXAMPLE **1.** Please let me know. My VCR is ready. To be picked up. *Please let me know when my VCR is ready to be picked up.*

Dear Manager:

The VCR repaired at your shop is not working properly. At all. When I try to tape a television show. The show on the tape is not the right one. Apparently the channels have been wrongly set. I am getting channels from cities. Strange cities that the TV has never picked up before. I have tapes of dog shows and cooking shows and sporting events that no one in this house. Although I program the VCR carefully. When I play the tapes. Nothing is what it is supposed to be. My questions. Your work guaranteed? Can the problem be fixed?

_____

_____

_____

_____

_____

_____

_____

_____

_____

LANGUAGE HANDBOOK **9** SENTENCE STYLE

WORKSHEET 6 | **Avoiding Run-on Sentences (Rule 9 e)**

EXERCISE A Correct each run-on sentence in three different ways: (1) Separate the independent clauses with a period, and start the second clause with a capital letter; (2) create a compound sentence by adding a coordinating conjunction and a comma; and (3) create a compound sentence by using a semicolon to connect the two independent clauses. Write only the words that come before and after the period, conjunction, or semicolon. On the first line, write *C* for any sentence that is not a run-on sentence.

EXAMPLES **1.** There is a category of words called group nouns, they are interesting.
_____nouns. They_____   _____nouns, **and** they_____   _____nouns; they_____

2. Many of the group nouns, but not all, describe animals.
_____C_____   _____   _____

1. Each kind of animal is referred to by a different group noun, it is often strange.

_____   _____   _____

2. A group of lions is called a pride, that's a pretty descriptive term.

_____   _____   _____

3. A group of whales is called a pod, I'm not sure why.

_____   _____   _____

4. Usually a group of birds is called a flock, but not all groups of them are.

_____   _____   _____

5. A group of geese on the ground is a gaggle, in flight it is called a skein.

_____   _____   _____

6. A group of sheep is often called a herd, it can also be called a mob.

_____   _____   _____

7. Fish come in schools, they change direction all together.

_____   _____   _____

8. Several monkeys make a troupe, maybe they are given that name because they are acrobats.

_____   _____   _____

9. Wolves make up a pack, just as cards do.

_____   _____   _____

10. It's fun to make up a descriptive group noun, such as a "cacophony of motorcycles."

_____   _____   _____

Continued ☞

EXERCISE B   Correct each run-on sentence in two ways: (1) by starting a new sentence and (2) by inserting a semicolon. Write only the words before and after the punctuation mark. On the first line provided, write *C* for each sentence that is not a run-on sentence.

EXAMPLES **1.** The weather was bad, consequently, the meeting was poorly attended.
bad. Consequently   *bad; Consequently*

2. If you cannot follow the plot of a movie, then you will lose interest.
_____ *C* _____   _____

1. Grandmother is interested in our family's history, therefore, she plans to revisit Turkey this fall.

_____   _____

2. I don't agree with Louis, nevertheless, I am willing to listen to his ideas.

_____   _____

3. An empty bottle is not really empty it is actually full of air.

_____   _____

4. If you don't show interest in your own speech, then nobody else will.

_____   _____

5. Many roads are made of asphalt, which is a byproduct of petroleum.

_____   _____

6. The poet Pablo Neruda was born in Chile subsequently, he lived in many other countries, including Burma and Spain.

_____   _____

7. Fortunately the warehouse fire occurred at night, otherwise, many lives might have been lost.

_____   _____

8. It is a new product, and, consequently, many people have never heard of it.

_____   _____

9. The lights flickered during the storm then they went out completely.

_____   _____

10. People who live in moderate climates use fireplaces mainly for decoration, however, people who live in colder climates use them for heat.

_____   _____

| WORSKHEET 7 | **Avoiding Unnecessary Shifts in Sentences; Varying Sentence Beginnings and Structure (Rules 9 f–h)** |

EXERCISE A   On the line provided, revise each of the following sentences to correct any unnecessary shifts in tense, voice, or subject. If the sentence contains a shift that is necessary to express its meaning and therefore needs no change, write *C*.

EXAMPLE **1.** Nina picked the peaches, and then she makes the pie. _Nina picked the peaches, and then she made the pie._

1. Dario, when can you climb up on the roof and be nailing down the loose shingles? _____

2. Sailing is fun and challenging, but you need some training. _____

3. Many people speak of Africa and South America as countries, but they were defined by my teachers as continents. _____

4. The manatee soon surfaced and is eating the lettuce. _____

5. The storm came in, and soon several inches of rain had fallen. _____

6. All desks were cleared off before two o'clock so that the art project can begin. _____

7. Faith reads Toni Morrison's books because the author's figurative language is fascinating to her.

8. The Zuni jewelry is inlaid with turquoise, coral, and the Zuni also use some other stones in the jewelry. _____

9. The trail was steep, and the horses' hooves slip and slide. _____

10. The computer needs to be unplugged whenever you will see lightning. _____

EXERCISE B   On the lines provided, revise each of the following sentences by using a variety of beginnings. The hint in parentheses will tell you which type of beginning to use. You may add or delete words or change word forms or order as needed.

EXAMPLE **1.** The cat pounced on the catnip mouse. (*phrase*) _With speed and cunning, the cat pounced on the catnip mouse._

Continued ☞

1. F. Scott Fitzgerald realized his dream of riches and fame and then was destroyed by his inability to cope with his success. (*single word modifier*) _____

_____

2. Isaac Bashevis Singer was born in Poland in 1904 and later lived in New York, where he pursued a career as a writer of stories, novels, and plays. (*clause*) _____

_____

3. Margaret Walker used poetry to celebrate the aspirations and struggles of African Americans and to relate black history to legend. (*clause*) _____

_____

4. Flannery O'Connor is a noted Southern writer whose stories capture her strong personal beliefs and her sense of what is important in the life around her. (*phrase*) _____

_____

5. James Thurber wrote stories and essays and drew cartoons that expressed his sense of humor about men, women, and dogs. (*phrase*) _____

_____

EXERCISE C Revise the following paragraph to create variety in sentence structure.

Baron De La Warr's name gave the English language the word *Delaware*. Baron De La Warr was an English colonial governor of Virginia from 1610 to 1611. He was known as Lord Delaware. The name Delaware was taken as the name of the first of the original thirteen colonies to become a state. The name is also applied to a river and a bay on the east coast of the United States. The name Delaware also was given to an Algonquian group of American Indians. They lived in the Delaware River valley.

_____

_____

_____

_____

_____

_____

_____

_____

_____

LANGUAGE HANDBOOK 9 SENTENCE STYLE

WORKSHEET 8 **Reducing Wordiness (Rule 9 i)**

EXERCISE A Revise each of the following sentences by making the italicized clause the type of phrase or clause indicated in parentheses. Add or delete any words as necessary to make the change.

ellip. = elliptical clause
part. = participial phrase
inf. = infinitive phrase

EXAMPLES **1.** I got the idea for this story *while I was peeling potatoes.* (*ellip.*)
I got the idea for this story while peeling potatoes.

2. *As he approached the curve*, the driver slowed down. (*part.*)
Approaching the curve, the driver slowed down.

3. We need a sign *that will attract attention.* (*inf.*) *We need a sign to attract attention.*

1. *If it is properly trained*, a dog will not chase cars. (*part.*) _____
_____
_____

2. Charlayne Hunter-Gault is very serious *when she is discussing politics.* (*ellip.*) _____
_____
_____

3. *Because she knew that I liked animals*, Aunt Jenny gave me a puppy for my birthday. (*part.*)
_____
_____

4. I lost my balance *while I was climbing the ladder.* (*ellip.*) _____
_____
_____

5. Mrs. Barry served us corn *that was raised in her own garden.* (*part.*) _____
_____
_____

6. The player *who holds the highest card* plays first. (*part.*) _____
_____
_____

7. I said nothing *that could have hurt Pedro's feelings.* (*inf.*) _____
_____
_____

Continued ☞

8. Francis Scott Key wrote "The Star-Spangled Banner" *while he was on a ship in Baltimore Harbor near Fort McHenry.* (*ellip.*) _____

_____

_____

9. Key's verses, *which were set to an eighteenth-century English song*, were written in 1814. (*part.*) _____

_____

_____

10. A bill *that was signed by President Hoover* in 1931 made "The Star-Spangled Banner" our official national anthem. (*part.*) _____

_____

_____

EXERCISE B   Revise each of the following sentences by reducing each italicized phrase or clause to the construction indicated in parentheses. Add, delete, or move any words as necessary to make this change.

> *prep.* = prepositional phrase
> *ger.* = gerund phrase
> *app.* = appositive
> *adj.* = adjective
> *adv.* = adverb

EXAMPLES **1.** Herodotus, *who wrote the first narrative history*, is often called "the father of history." (*app.*) _Herodotus, writer of the first narrative history, is often called "the father of history."_

2. Even the people *who were in the last row* heard very well. (*prep.*) _Even the people in the last row heard very well._

3. We were stuck for an hour on a road *that was muddy*. (*adj.*) _We were stuck for an hour on a muddy road._

4. Georgia O'Keeffe depicted all her subjects *with care*. (*adv.*) _Georgia O'Keeffe carefully depicted all her subjects._

5. I believe in *the prevention of accidents* before they happen. (*ger.*) _I believe in preventing accidents before they happen._

1. A singer *whose voice was very good* sang several blues songs. (*prep.*) _____

_____

_____

Continued ☞

2. There are telephones *for the public* in the hotel lobby. (*adj.*) _____

_____

_____

3. You can't do the job *in a satisfactory way* in ten minutes. (*adv.*) _____

_____

_____

4. The Red Cross immediately sent help to the disaster area *that was in India*. (*prep.*) _____

_____

_____

5. Galileo, *who was an Italian astronomer*, offered proof that Earth revolves around the Sun. (*app.*) _____

_____

_____

6. The committee suggested a new plan for *the reduction of air pollution*. (*ger.*) _____

_____

_____

7. The country of San Marino is well known to stamp collectors for *the creation of beautiful postage stamps*. (*ger.*) _____

_____

_____

8. The family has always been responsible *in financial matters*. (*adv.*) _____

_____

_____

9. The actress gave no explanation for *why she left the show*. (*ger.*) _____

_____

_____

10. We finally decided to enroll our dog in a school *that teaches obedience*. (*adj.*) _____

_____

_____

WORKSHEET 9 | Test (Rules 9 a–i)

EXERCISE A For each of the following word groups, write the coordinating or subordinating conjunction that most clearly expresses the relationship between each pair of ideas. Then, circle the *C* or the *S* to show whether you have used *coordination* or *subordination*. You do not need to capitalize or punctuate the word groups for this exercise.

EXAMPLES Ⓒ S **1.** We saw the approaching truck, ___*but*___ the driver failed to see us.

C Ⓢ **2.** ___*As*___ we left our hotel, the town was beginning to awake for the day's business.

C S **1.** _____ the Maya had no clocks or telescopes, they could predict solar and lunar eclipses.

C S **2.** _____ the children left, our house seemed unusually quiet.

C S **3.** Herb nominated Elsa _____ Elsa nominated Herb.

C S **4.** Many people feel sad _____ they see a beautiful tree cut down.

C S **5.** _____ we do not go together, we can meet in the lobby of the theater.

C S **6.** The American Indians had never seen horses _____ the Spanish brought them to this continent.

C S **7.** The seeds failed to germinate _____ they had been planted too deep.

C S **8.** I would have introduced you to my acquaintance, _____ I had forgotten his name.

C S **9.** The festival is always exciting _____ the Teatro Flamenco is onstage.

C S **10.** Mayor Stack was an ardent supporter of Councilman Suarez, _____ the voters reelected the councilman by a wide margin.

EXERCISE B On the line provided, combine the following sentences by coordinating or subordinating ideas.

EXAMPLE **1.** The birdbath was being filled. The birds waited on the fence.
While the birdbath was being filled, the birds waited on the fence.

1. The electricity was turned off. The payment was late. _____

_____

_____

2. The goal of the committee is to recommend green spaces in the city. Green spaces should be set aside and protected. _____

_____

_____

Continued ☞

3. My favorite poet is Leslie Marmon Silko. She is of Laguna, Mexican, and European ancestry. __

_____

_____

4. The shoreline is receding each year. Our beach house is not in jeopardy. _____

_____

_____

5. Tanya checks the stock market quotes every morning. She is thinking about selling one
hundred shares. _____

_____

_____

6. A ceremony marked the dedication of the new club. A large crowd attended. _____

_____

_____

7. Darrell was not late for his appointment. He was a day early. _____

_____

_____

8. El Paso is in the United States. Juárez, its neighboring city, is in Mexico. _____

_____

_____

9. The ad said that only experienced people need apply. I have plenty of the experience needed
for the job. _____

_____

_____

10. You can go to the bank and the post office. While you are doing that, I will go to the grocery
store. _____

_____

_____

EXERCISE C   On the lines provided, create complete sentences from the fragments given.

> **EXAMPLE 1.** Sifting through the ashes. The lost coin. _Sifting through the_
> _ashes, we found the lost coin._

1. In our front yard one morning and wouldn't go away. A dog appearing. _____

_____

_____

Continued ☞

2. The ancient Anasazi people. To build intricate pueblo cities. _____

_____

_____

3. Avoid stress in your life. Necessary that you follow a proper diet. _____

_____

_____

4. The recycling center. Purchasing a new paper compactor. Better serve the county. _____

_____

_____

5. The weather so unpredictable. Carrying an umbrella and boots in my car. _____

_____

_____

EXERCISE D   On the lines provided, revise the following sentences by using parallel structure.

> EXAMPLE **1.** I planned to go to college and will major in computer science.
> *I planned to go to college and major in computer science.*

1. Beverly sings beautifully, and intricate needlework is done by her. _____

_____

_____

2. My friends and I planned to go to the amusement park, and later we will watch a video at my house. _____

_____

_____

3. Juan hopes that the experiment will work and to present it at the science fair. _____

_____

_____

4. Black Hawk was not only a great warrior, but also with skills as an orator. _____

_____

_____

5. To write clearly is as important as thinking clearly. _____

_____

_____

Continued ☞

EXERCISE E   Divide the following word groups into sentences. Then, rewrite the word groups, inserting any necessary end marks and capital letters.

> EXAMPLE **1.** On Halloween night in 1938, people in the United States received a scare when Orson Welles broadcast H. G. Wells's *The War of the Worlds* in this thriller Martian invaders arrive in a huge flying cylinder and start to lay waste to the countryside. *On Halloween night in 1938, people in the United States received a scare when Orson Welles broadcast H. G. Wells's The War of the Worlds. In this thriller Martian invaders arrive in a huge flying cylinder and start to lay waste to the countryside.*

1. Radio listeners who had tuned in at the beginning of the program had heard the announcement that the Mercury Theater was about to dramatize Wells's tale the realistic program was, however, a terrifying experience for those who tuned in after it had started. ____

_____

_____

_____

2. Spinning their dials unsuspectingly, they came across this program, which was made to sound like a live news broadcast two cities, Chicago and St. Louis, were reported to have been bombed there were alarming reports from people supposedly on the scene of the disaster and simulated warnings from public officials. _____

_____

_____

_____

3. Newspaper offices and police stations were swamped with telephone calls traffic was tied up by ambulances, police cars, and fire engines rushing to the rescue of victims fifteen people were treated for shock and heart attacks at a hospital in Newark. _____

_____

_____

_____

4. The Associated Press sent a bulletin assuring the public that the broadcast was merely a story Orson Welles claimed that the scare was unintentional and that he had feared that the old story might not even interest a modern audience. _____

_____

_____

_____

_____

Continued ☞

EXERCISE F   On the lines provided, rewrite each of the following sentences to correct unnecessary shifts in subject, verb tense, and voice. If a sentence is already correct, write *C*.

> EXAMPLE **1.** I appreciate nature, and animals are considered special by me.
> *I appreciate nature and consider animals special.*

1. I like to get up early in the morning and go to the meadow so that one can see wild turkeys.

_____

_____

2. I usually walked quietly around the pond and stand behind the blackberry bushes. _____

_____

_____

3. I look in the meadow, and a wonderful sight is shown to me. _____

_____

_____

4. I see about two dozen turkeys feeding in the early morning light. _____

_____

_____

5. I knew that next I will see the turkeys fly in a flock out of the meadow and over the pond. ___

_____

_____

EXERCISE G   Use the corrected sentences in Exercise F above to write a paragraph on the lines provided. Vary sentence beginnings and sentence structures. Begin at least one sentence with each of the following: a participial phrase, a prepositional phrase, and an adverb clause. Include at least one of each of the following sentence structures: simple, compound, complex, and compound-complex.

_____

_____

_____

_____

_____

_____

_____

_____

_____

_____

_____

Continued ☞

LANGUAGE HANDBOOK 9 WORSHEET 9 *(continued)*

EXERCISE H Revise the following sentences by crossing out any unnecessary words. Then, on the lines provided, rewrite each sentence to make it as clear and concise as possible.

> EXAMPLE 1. Chinua Achebe's first novel, *Things Fall Apart*, dramatizes
> traditional Ibo life ~~and is set in an Ibo~~ village in Nigeria. *Chinua*
> *Achebe's first novel, Things Fall Apart, dramatizes traditional Ibo*
> *village life in Nigeria.*

1. The gale damaged trees more than it did damage to houses. _____
_____

2. Except for the country with the largest population in the world, China, India has the largest population in the world. _____
_____
_____

3. Field hockey is a game that always keeps you in suspense at all times. _____
_____

4. In the year 1907, the psychiatrist Carl Jung met Sigmund Freud, and Jung became Freud's student who followed him for several years after that. _____
_____
_____

5. Jung sought to classify human beings by dividing them into categories according to different types of temperaments that varied one from another. _____
_____
_____

6. Jung's first, and what is his best-known, distinction that he made was between the extroverted and introverted temperaments. _____
_____
_____

7. There is a great deal of danger connected with mountain climbing. _____
_____

8. Noises that are sudden and loud have always had the effect of causing me great fright. _____
_____

9. Before the realization of what had happened came to me, it was too late. _____
_____

10. Felicia receives pleasure when she does paintings that depict scenes containing incidents from the lives of the gods and goddesses of ancient Greece. _____
_____
_____

LANGUAGE HANDBOOK 10 SENTENCE COMBINING

| WORKSHEET 1 | **Using Adjectives, Adverbs, and Prepositional Phrases to Combine Sentences (Rules 10 a, b)** |

EXERCISE A   Combine each group of sentences into one sentence by building upon the first sentence and by eliminating needless words. Use adjectives, adverbs, and prepositional phrases to combine the sentences. Be sure to punctuate your sentences correctly.

EXAMPLE **1.** Mr. and Mrs. Levy live in a small cottage. The cottage is white. They live comfortably. The cottage is near Cranberry Lake. _____
Mr. and Mrs. Levy live comfortably in a small, white cottage near _____
Cranberry Lake. _____

1. It becomes cold in the Adirondack region. It becomes cold in the winter. It often becomes extremely cold. _____

_____

_____

2. In several mountain regions, snowfall is heavy. The regions are east of the Mississippi. The snowfall is heavy this year. _____

_____

_____

3. The northwest wind brings temperatures down. It brings temperatures down to below 0˚F. It brings temperatures down at night. _____

_____

_____

4. Students inspect the pines. They are students in the forestry school. The pines are huge. They are inspected for storm damage. _____

_____

_____

5. Nara stokes her iron stove. It is in the living room. She stokes the stove with firewood. The firewood is from a nearby pine grove. _____

_____

_____

EXERCISE B   Combine the following groups of sentences by changing the italicized sentence to an appositive phrase. Remember to use commas to set off each appositive phrase.

EXAMPLE **1.** Stephen Crane died when he was only twenty-eight. *He was the author of "The Open Boat."* *Stephen Crane, the author of "The* _____
Open Boat," died when he was only twenty-eight. _____

1. "The Open Boat" is based on his personal experience. *It is a story about a shipwreck.* _____

_____

Continued ☞

2. Stephen Crane had thirteen brothers and sisters. *He was the son of a Methodist minister.*___

_____

_____

3. Crane shocked his college English professor by criticizing Tennyson. *Tennyson was a popular English poet.* _____

_____

_____

4. Crane played shortstop on the varsity baseball team at college. *Crane was a good athlete.*___

_____

_____

5. During his career Stephen Crane traveled to Mexico, Cuba, and Greece. *These countries were the scenes of fierce fighting.* _____

_____

_____

6. He lived in England and became a good friend of Joseph Conrad. *Conrad is the author of "The Secret Sharer."* _____

_____

_____

7. Texas is the locale of one of Crane's best short stories. *The story is "The Bride Comes to Yellow Sky."* _____

_____

_____

8. Crane's masterpiece is *The Red Badge of Courage. It is a novel about the Civil War.* _____

_____

_____

9. Two writers of his time praised his work. *The writers were Hamlin Garland and William Dean Howells.* _____

_____

_____

10. Accurate details in the novel show the gruesome aspects of war. *The details were the result of careful research by Crane.* _____

_____

_____

| WORSHEET 2 | **Using Participial Phrases to Combine Sentences (Rule 10 b)** |

EXERCISE A   Combine each pair of sentences by making one of the sentences a participial phrase. Punctuate the combined sentence correctly.

> **EXAMPLE** **1.** Pete handed the composition to Elaine. He praised its clear, readable style. _Pete handed the composition to Elaine, praising its clear, readable style._

1. *The Tale of Genji* is believed to be the world's first novel. It was written by Murasaki Shikibu around A.D. 1000. _____

_____

_____

2. Inez rode her bicycle to the store. She was pedaling furiously. _____

_____

3. I reached into the water. I grabbed the fish by the tail. _____

_____

4. The Egyptians invented hieroglyphic writing about 3500–3000 B.C. This writing was inscribed on the tombs of the pharaohs. _____

_____

_____

5. We stood at the bus stop. We waited for the bus to arrive. _____

_____

6. The smoke indicated that the house was occupied. The smoke was billowing from the chimney. _____

_____

7. In class we saw the movie *Les Misérables*. It was based on the novel by Victor Hugo. _____

_____

8. Everyone listened to the talented girl. She was playing the dulcimer. _____

_____

9. For many animals the Santee Swamp in South Carolina is a haven. These animals are endangered by extinction. _____

_____

_____

10. Francis Marion's troops waged guerrilla war against the British during the Revolutionary War. The troops often hid in the Santee Swamp. _____

_____

_____

Continued ☞

LANGUAGE HANDBOOK 10 WORSHEET 2 *(continued)*

EXERCISE B   Combine the following sentence pairs by making some part of the italicized sentence a participial phrase. Punctuate the combined sentence correctly.

EXAMPLE   **1.** The Aswan High Dam is in Egypt. *It was completed in 1968.* <u>The Aswan High Dam, completed in 1968, is in Egypt.</u>

1. Juanita wore a rebozo. *It was borrowed from a friend.* _____

_____

2. We stood in the doorway. *We waited for the rain to stop.* _____

_____

3. Liang circulated among his guests. *He chatted a moment with each one.* _____

_____

_____

4. The guides are high school students. *They are dressed in Colonial costume.* _____

_____

_____

5. *I attempted to start a conversation.* I made a remark about the weather. _____

_____

_____

6. *The entire stock was damaged by smoke and water.* It was reduced in price. _____

_____

_____

7. *A violin weighs about a pound.* It consists of about seventy pieces. _____

_____

_____

8. *The company anticipated a shortage.* It bought large amounts of steel. _____

_____

_____

9. The barracuda will attack a person. *It is called the tiger of the sea.* _____

_____

_____

10. *The movie was adapted from a popular novel by Harper Lee.* It strikes a blow against intolerance. _____

_____

_____

LANGUAGE HANDBOOK **10** **SENTENCE COMBINING**

| WORSHEET 3 | **Using Phrases to Combine Sentences (Rule 10 b)**

EXERCISE A   Combine the following sentence pairs by changing part of the italicized sentence to an infinitive phrase.

EXAMPLE **1.** Zora Neale Hurston left New York City for Mobile, Alabama. *She planned to collect examples of African American folklore.* <u>Zora Neale Hurston left New York City for Mobile, Alabama, to collect examples of African American folklore.</u>

1. Georgetown, Texas, has a plan. *It will attract new industries.* _____

_____

_____

2. The Osaka Restaurant buys miso and rice in large quantities. *In this way it gets a better price.*

_____

_____

3. *Don't leave the car motor running.* It wastes gas and pollutes the air. _____

_____

_____

4. I wrote down the figures. *This would prevent any misunderstanding.* _____

_____

_____

5. Thoreau took to the woods. *He wanted to learn how simply he could live.* _____

_____

_____

6. We sent out cards. *They reminded people to vote.* _____

_____

_____

7. You must read the novels of Gabriel García Márquez. *You will understand his use of magical realism.* _____

_____

_____

8. Jane Austen wrote her novels in a corner of the drawing room. *She wished to avoid the disapproval of her relatives.* _____

_____

_____

Continued ☞

9. Virginia Woolf said that a woman needs a room of her own. *There she can write in undisturbed privacy.* _____

_____

_____

10. In recent years people in the United States have developed conservation methods. *These methods save energy.* _____

_____

_____

EXERCISE B Combine the following sentence pairs by changing part of the italicized sentence to a gerund phrase. Add or rearrange words as necessary.

EXAMPLE **1.** *I read Adrienne Rich's poem "Meditations for a Savage Child."* This made me curious about stories of children raised by animals.
Reading Adrienne Rich's poem "Meditations for a Savage Child" made me curious about stories of children raised by animals.

1. The bus company has a machine for coins. *It sorts out coins.* _____

_____

_____

_____

2. *Read your theme aloud.* It is a good test for clarity and style. _____

_____

_____

_____

3. Jill has an annoying habit of doing something. *She leaves doors open.* _____

_____

_____

_____

4. *The dog chewed its leash in two.* It escaped from the yard by doing so. _____

_____

_____

_____

5. *I lost my receipt.* This loss caused me great inconvenience. _____

_____

_____

_____

Elements of Literature

WORKSHEET 4 | **Combining Sentences by Coordinating Ideas (Rule 10 c)**

EXERCISE A   Combine each sentence group into one sentence by using coordinating conjunctions. Punctuate your combined sentence correctly.

> EXAMPLE **1.** Michael played on the hockey team. He never scored a goal.
> _Michael played on the hockey team, but he never scored a goal._

1. Rhonda's father once played professional hockey. Her uncle once played it, too. _____
_____

2. Everyone in the Park family likes athletics. Everyone participates in the annual 10K Fun Run.
_____
_____

3. Mike works hard in chemistry to get good grades. He works hard in English, too. _____
_____

4. He is considering being an accountant. He is also considering being a doctor. _____
_____

5. Mary Karr is an interesting writer. She has made writing her career. _____
_____

6. Running is an excellent means for keeping in shape. Swimming is also an excellent means for keeping in shape. _____
_____
_____

7. The flower shop is open during the day. It is closed on most evenings. _____
_____

8. On Saturdays I prepare breakfast for my family. My brother makes lunch. We both help Mother cook dinner. _____
_____
_____

9. Sinta knows how to make flat Javanese shadow puppets. Luís knows how as well. They are planning a puppet show for the Children's Fair. _____
_____
_____

10. Melissa will drive the car to the train station. She will pick up the rest of the family. Her sister will stay at the house. _____
_____
_____

Continued ☞

LANGUAGE HANDBOOK 10 WORSHEET 4 *(continued)*

EXERCISE B On the line provided, use a coordinating conjunction, a correlative conjunction, a conjunctive adverb and a semicolon, or a semicolon to combine each set of related sentences.

EXAMPLE **1.** The elevator was closed for repair. We had to use the stairs instead. *The elevator was closed for repair; therefore, we had to use the stairs instead.*

1. A small leak in the aquarium turned into a big one. All of the fish had to be removed and put into other tanks. _____

_____

2. Many people do not understand astrophysics. Many do not understand quantum mechanics.

_____

3. Claude McKay is a famous African American poet. Countee Cullen is a famous African American poet. _____

_____

4. We bought two cartons of raspberries. We also bought two gallons of blueberries. _____

_____

5. Sandra's truck ran out of gas on the highway. She flagged down a passer-by for help. _____

_____

6. Winona enjoys bowling. She doesn't want to join a league. _____

_____

7. Roberto was born in Puerto Rico. He has lived most of his life in the Dominican Republic.____

_____

8. Sewing buttons on shirts may be easy. I've never done it. _____

_____

9. Ms. Angelis may buy a new car. She may instead go on a tour of Spain. _____

10. The children finished their T-ball season. It was a successful year for their team. _____

_____

LANGUAGE HANDBOOK **10** **SENTENCE COMBINING**

WORKSHEET 5 | ## Using Adjective Clauses to Combine Sentences (Rule 10 d)

EXERCISE A   Combine each of the following pairs of sentences by making one sentence an adjective clause. Punctuate the combined sentence correctly. There may be more than one correct way to revise these sentence pairs.

EXAMPLE **1.** This book begins with several chapters on linear functions. It may help you review for the test. _This book, which begins with several chapters on linear functions, may help you review for the test._

or

This book, which may help you review for the test, begins with several chapters on linear functions.

1. The community center was paid for by Mrs. Wang. She also donated her Chinese art collection to the local museum. _____

2. Commander Elkins was awarded a medal for his bravery. He fought in three of our country's wars. _____

3. The students enjoyed the Comanche gourd dancing workshop. It was presented by Mr. Kosechata and Ms. Pewa. _____

4. I want you to meet Bruce. He is the captain of the debate team. _____

5. The answer was really quite simple. No one could guess it. _____

6. A causeway is being built. It will cross the swampy area. _____

7. Veronica is one of the candidates. Her friends call her Ronnie. _____

8. African American engineer Granville T. Woods obtained at least fifty patents. He received his first patent in 1884. _____

9. A thesaurus is a handy tool for a writer. It lists synonyms for many words. _____

10. Tiwa mentioned the name of a football player. We had not heard of him before. _____

Continued ☞

LANGUAGE HANDBOOK **10** **WORKSHEET 5** *(continued)*

EXERCISE B   Combine each pair of sentences by changing the italicized sentence to an adjective clause. Be sure to put the clause next to the word it modifies. *Note:* Nonessential clauses require commas; essential clauses do not.

> **EXAMPLES** **1.** The wallet was returned. *I lost it yesterday.* <u>The wallet that I lost yesterday was returned.</u>
>
> **2.** The room has two doors. *One of them is always locked.* <u>The room has two doors, one of which is always locked.</u>

1. The sofa arrived today. *We ordered it last month.* _____

_____

_____

2. Phillis Wheatley lived in Boston. *She was the first African American writer to publish a book of poetry.* _____

_____

_____

3. The sailboat suddenly capsized. *I had been watching it.* _____

_____

_____

4. The students were late to class. *They had been working on the stage.* _____

_____

_____

5. Grandmother Tallchief has a friend. *She plays chess with her.* _____

_____

_____

6. The woman received one hundred dollars. *Her question stumped the experts.* ____

_____

_____

7. I have a friend. *His father is an astronaut.* _____

_____

8. Our pastor told a story. *I have always remembered it.* _____

_____

9. We came to a bridge. *Some people were fishing on it.* _____

_____

10. I have two brothers. *Both of them study Japanese Noh and Kabuki drama.* ____

_____

_____

Elements of Literature

WORKSHEET 6 | **Using Adverb Clauses and Noun Clauses to Combine Sentences (Rule 10 d)**

EXERCISE A   Combine each of the following pairs of sentences by making one sentence an adverb clause. You will need to add a subordinating conjunction that expresses the relationship between the sentences. Eliminate any needless words. Punctuate the combined sentence correctly. There may be more than one correct way to combine these sentence pairs.

> EXAMPLE   **1.** Glaciers covered part of North America. They extended as far south as the Ohio River Valley. *When glaciers covered part of North America, they extended as far south as the Ohio River Valley.*

1. Dr. Ralph Bunche earned his Ph.D. from Harvard University. He became the first African American to receive the Nobel Peace Prize. _____

_____

2. Tranh comes to visit now and then. He brings his guitar. _____

_____

3. You were writing letters. At the same time, I was making phone calls. _____

_____

4. We began our discussion of the Tahitian and Maori languages. Just then, the bell rang. _____

_____

_____

5. Citizens will oppose building the fertilizer plant. They are concerned about water and air quality. _____

_____

_____

6. Charles Dickens traveled through the United States. He kept a journal. _____

_____

7. We will change the rules. Everyone can play. _____

_____

8. The cotton has not fully matured. Harvesting will be rescheduled. _____

_____

9. The rain had soaked the field. The umpires canceled the game. _____

_____

10. Alicia Alonso began to lose her eyesight at the age of nineteen. She danced and taught classical ballet for almost half a century. _____

_____

_____

Continued ☞

EXERCISE B   Combine each of the following pairs of sentences by making one sentence a noun clause. You may change the order of words, but do not change the meaning of the sentences. Punctuate your sentences correctly.

EXAMPLE **1.** The road to Marsabit goes through the jungle. We read this fact in the tour guide. _We read in the tour guide that the road to Marsabit goes through the jungle._

1. We could make the trip to Chichén Itzá in one day. We were not sure. _____

_____

_____

2. Breakfast is the most important meal of the day. Many people forget this fact. _____

_____

_____

3. For some reason, he slid into first base. Only he would know why. _____

_____

_____

4. All of the Branwells have gone to Europe. I found this out yesterday. _____

_____

_____

5. The boat left. We wanted to know when. _____

_____

6. She will win the triathlon. Everyone at the finish line expects it. _____

_____

7. We took first prize. There are two good explanations for this success. _____

_____

_____

8. Half of all books printed before the eighteenth century were published in Chinese. Most students do not know this. _____

_____

_____

9. He was about to try out for the part in _West Side Story_. He told us. _____

_____

_____

10. We collaborated on the essay. This fact was published in the school newspaper. _____

_____

_____

LANGUAGE HANDBOOK **10** **SENTENCE COMBINING**

| WORKSHEET 7 | Test (Rules 10 a–d)

EXERCISE A   Combine the independent clause in italics with the clauses printed in regular type to create a new sentence. Use the combined clauses as indicated in parentheses.

EXAMPLE   **1.** (a) *Ground glass is sprinkled on the highway lines*.

(b) The paint is still wet. (*adverb clause*)

(c) The glass reflects light at night. (*infinitive phrase*)

While the paint is still wet, ground glass is sprinkled on the highway lines to reflect light at night.

1. (a) *Judge Elizabeth Fry passed sentence on a man.*

(b) She was a strict jurist. (*appositive phrase*)

(c) He had continued to drive his car. (*adjective clause*)

(d) His license had been revoked. (*adverb clause*)

_____

_____

2. (a) *The winning photograph showed a group of basketball players.*

(b) They were "frozen" in midair. (*participial phrase*)

(c) They jumped for the ball. (*adverb clause*)

_____

_____

3. (a) *The children earned money for their class trip.*

(b) They earned money by the sale of old newspapers to recycling plants. (*gerund phrase*)

(c) They had collected the newspapers from their neighbors. (*adjective clause*)

_____

_____

4. (a) He was hunting rare plants in the jungles of Indochina. (*elliptical adverb clause*)

(b) *A French scientist discovered the ruins of a magnificent city.*

(c) It had been abandoned for centuries. (*adjective clause*)

_____

_____

Continued ☞

5. (a) Many people couldn't read. (*adverb clause*)

(b) *Merchants used to put up picture signs.*

(c) These would show what they had to sell. (*infinitive phrase*)

_____

_____

EXERCISE B   Combine the independent clause in italics with the clauses printed in regular type, adding or changing words when needed. Use the combined clauses as indicated in parentheses.

EXAMPLE   **1.** (a) *Lame ducks are public officials.*

(b) They are finishing out their terms. (*adjective clause*)

(c) They have run for reelection and been defeated. (*adverb clause*)

Lame ducks are public officials who are finishing out their terms
after they have run for reelection and been defeated.

1. (a) Dolley Madison was the First Lady. (*adverb clause*)

(b) *She served her guests a custard.*

(c) The custard was frozen. (*adjective*)

(d) It soon became popularly known as ice cream. (*adjective clause*)

_____

_____

2. (a) *A presidential train is always accompanied by a pilot train.*

(b) A pilot train is a locomotive with only one car. (*appositive phrase*)

(c) A pilot train travels just ahead of the president's train. (*adjective clause*)

(d) The purpose is to protect it. (*infinitive phrase*)

_____

_____

3. (a) *George Moore had a cat.*

(b) It forced him to pay attention to it. (*adjective clause*)

(c) It got his attention when it jumped onto his desk and when it took his pen from his hand. (*gerund phrase*)

(d) Moore was an Irish novelist. (*appositive*)

_____

_____

Continued ☞

LANGUAGE HANDBOOK **10** **WORKSHEET 7** *(continued)*

4. (a) This invention was made in the eighteenth century. (*prepositional phrase*)

(b) *A Dutchman invented roller skates.*

(c) He attached wheels to his ice skates. (*gerund phrase*)

(d) He could skate in warm weather. (*adverb clause*)

_____

_____

5. (a) *The first airplane flight from a ship took place in 1910.*

(b) Eugene Ely flew a land plane from a temporary wooden runway. (*adverb clause*)

(c) He was a pioneering pilot. (*appositive phrase*)

(d) The runway was constructed on the deck of the USS *Birmingham*. (*participial phrase*)

_____

_____

_____

EXERCISE C   Revise the following paragraph, combining sentences where possible. Add, delete, or rearrange words to make the paragraph read smoothly. Punctuate your revised paragraph correctly.

Pearl Buck spent her childhood in China. She wrote many books. These books are based on her experiences there. *The Good Earth* is the most famous of these books. It is a story about Chinese farm life. Pearl Buck is known for something besides her writing. She is known for her devotion to children. She adopted several children. Some of them had disabilities. She lived with these children on a large farm in Pennsylvania. She also tried to find homes for other children. Many of these children were Asian orphans.

_____

_____

_____

_____

_____

_____

_____

_____

_____

_____

_____

LANGUAGE HANDBOOK	**11**	**CAPITALIZATION**

WORKSHEET 1 **Capitalizing First Words, Proper Nouns, and Proper Adjectives (Rules 11 a–d)**

EXERCISE A   Draw a line through each lowercase letter that should be a capital letter. Then, write the capital letter above it.

> **EXAMPLE 1.** Many ~~c~~hinese and ~~j~~apanese live in the ~~h~~awaiian ~~i~~slands.
> <small>C   J   H   I</small>

1. When ~~harlem~~ was settled by the ~~dutch~~, it comprised all the land north of what is now fifty-ninth street, from the east river to the hudson river.

2. Today this area of uptown manhattan is bounded by fifth avenue on the east and the hudson river on the west.

3. The other four boroughs of new york include the bronx, brooklyn, queens, and Staten island.

4. the neighborhood below houston street is known as soho.

5. During world war I, people from the south started to come north in large numbers to get jobs in the booming wartime industries.

EXERCISE B   In the following letter, draw a line through any lowercase letter that should be capitalized and write the correct capital letter above it.

> **EXAMPLE** [1] ~~e~~nclosed is the information you requested.
> <small>E</small>

[1] dear Mr. Carrington,

[2] you asked us students to tell you which literary selections made a strong impression on us this year. [3] at first, I didn't think I would like much of the literature in our textbook, but I did, in fact, enjoy it. [4] not only did I like much of what we read, but also it tied in nicely with my american history class. [5] the excerpt from Thomas paine's famous pamphlet *The Crisis, No. 1* made me feel the revolutionary fervor that compelled many patriots to fight for independence. [6] especially forceful is the essay's opening line: "these are the times that try men's souls." [7] another selection that helped bring an era of american history to life for me was the last line of randall jarrell's poem "The Death of the Ball Turret Gunner": "when I died they washed me out of the turret with a hose." [8] this is a graphic image of the high price of war and freedom; it will stay with me a long time. [9] in retrospect, I have learned quite a bit about the literature and history of our country this year.

[10] sincerely,

Kevin

LANGUAGE
HANDBOOK **11** CAPITALIZATION

WORKSHEET 2 | **Capitalizing First Words, Proper Nouns and Adjectives, and School Subjects (Rules 11 a–e)**

EXERCISE A In the following sentences, draw a line through each lowercase letter that should be capitalized and write the correct capital letter above it.

EXAMPLES [1] ~~e~~nclosed is a list of my personal references. [2] ~~p~~lease add it to my file.

[1] dear ms. rivera:

[2] i am applying for the position of assistant at blue mountain kennels. [3] as my résumé indicates, I have extensive experience in dog training: in fact, several of the animals I have trained have won competitions. [4] i have worked with several breeds recognized by the american kennel club, including irish setters, brittany spaniels, and german shepherds. [5] currently, I am working for dr. Carl welch, a veterinarian in madison, wisconsin. [6] his practice, route 10 vet clinic, is for both large and small animals. [7] i am interested in relocating to the southwest, however, because I intend to apply to veterinary school in arizona. [8] since I speak spanish fluently, I can help out in the front office as well as work with the dogs. [9] i look forward to hearing from you soon.

[10] cordially yours,

nancy green

EXERCISE B In the following sentences, draw a line through each lowercase letter that should be capitalized and write the correct capital letter above it.

EXAMPLE **1.** The place that serves that delicious sandwich is called ~~m~~oe's.

1. Is *titanic* the name not only of a ship but also of a movie?
2. do you want me to buy freshflow orange juice or a generic brand?
3. my brother wants to join the united states navy after he graduates.
4. the boggy creek organic food festival takes place right after labor day.
5. the great depression of the 1930s was followed by world war II.
6. dad surprised me with a new computers united printer for my birthday.
7. do you wonder if there are any martians on mars or plutonians on pluto?
8. We learned about the big dipper constellation in astronomy 101.
9. sioux hunters once roamed the vast prairies in search of buffalo.
10. could we celebrate my birthday by eating at toby's taco hut?

LANGUAGE HANDBOOK **11** **CAPITALIZATION**

WORKSHEET 3 | **Capitalizing Proper Nouns, Proper Adjectives, School Subjects, and Titles (Rules 11 c–e)**

EXERCISE A   In the following sentences, draw a line through each letter that should be capitalized. Then, write the correct capital letter above it.

>   A   A   T
> **EXAMPLE 1.** James Stewart won an *A*cademy *A*ward for his performance in *t*he
>   P   S
>   *p*hiladelphia *s*tory.

1. The Monroe doctrine established the united states's sphere of influence in the western hemisphere.

2. Henry Wadsworth Longfellow wrote *the song of hiawatha*.

3. Did you know uncle William was a sergeant during world war II?

4. Many synagogues have services on both friday evening and saturday.

5. The owner of the *lakeland news* is supporting mayor Sanchez for re-election.

6. During the middle ages, the Ibo people of africa had a flourishing culture.

7. The apaches live in southern arizona, new mexico, and mexico.

8. R. H. Macy and company, inc., was started by a man from nantucket.

9. The sharpmobile automobile is cheaper in the midwest, according to dad.

10. Two students from Westhill high school wrote prize-winning essays about north american pioneers.

EXERCISE B   In the following sentences, draw a line through each lowercase letter that should be capitalized and write the correct capital letter above it.

>   J   E
> **EXAMPLE 1.** *j*essie is taking *e*nglish III, but he is not taking any math.

1. I was going to sign up for speech 101, but I decided to take photography instead.

2. My sister zoe bought a new compuquick computer to replace her old one.

3. I'd have to say american romanticism is my favorite literary period.

4. Pat mora wrote the poem "now and then, america."

5. Next year, our school will offer more computer science classes, but russian might be cut.

6. My uncle charlie is mom's only brother, but I have two other uncles on my father's side.

7. I plan to attend the university of iowa and major in biology.

8. Head north from seattle, and eventually you will reach the canadian wilderness.

9. I learned about the chinese new year in my world history class.

10. My friend's mom, mrs. stein, is teaching hebrew; the focus of the class is the Torah.

LANGUAGE HANDBOOK **11** **CAPITALIZATION**

WORKSHEET 4 | **Capitalizing Proper Nouns, Proper Adjectives, and Titles (Rules 11 c, e)**

EXERCISE A   In the following sentences, draw a line through each lowercase letter that should be capitalized and write the correct capital letter above it.

> EXAMPLE **1.** Julia Ward Howe published "*T*he *B*attle *H*ymn of the *R*epublic" in 1862.

1. The painting *fall plowing* by Grant Wood reminds me somewhat of a Grandma Moses painting.

2. *gone with the wind* is a movie that continues to capture the imagination of audiences everywhere.

3. The ninth month of the islamic year is called ramadan.

4. I called my doctor, who in turn referred me to sarita jones, m.d.

5. According to dad, buddhism teaches that suffering is inherent in life but that one can be liberated from it by self-purification.

6. My favorite magazine is *national geographic* because the writing is good, the maps are great, and the photography is outstanding.

7. Three hindu gods are vishnu, brahma, and siva.

8. Pat loves watching reruns of *the Brady Bunch*.

9. Thoreau's famous essay "civil disobedience" has inspired many people.

10. The first book of the bible is called genesis, which means "beginning" or "origin."

EXERCISE B   In the following sentences, draw a line through each incorrect capital or lowercase letter and write the correct form above it.

> EXAMPLE **1.** *M*r. *S*imon is a *d*octor who specializes in *p*ediatric *n*eurology.

1. The first President of the United States was general george washington.

2. *the grapes of wrath* is considered by many to be John steinbeck's masterpiece of American Fiction.

3. A Japanese Religion called shinto consists in the devotion to Deities of natural forces.

4. Ask grandma if we are going to meet at uncle bob's or my Mom's house.

5. The short-story collection *jungle tales* by horacio quiroga was published in 1918.

6. Mozart finished his Opera *don giovanni* in 1787.

7. I'm sure mom will remember the name of the previous Governor of Texas.

8. The book of psalms contains some verses that are thanksgivings or prayers of gratitude.

9. The Goddess of love in Greek mythology is called Aphrodite; venus is her name in Roman mythology.

10. The name of our catholic priest is father Callahan.

LANGUAGE HANDBOOK 11 CAPITALIZATION

WORKSHEET 5 Test (Rules 11 a–e)

EXERCISE A In the following sentences, draw a line through each lowercase letter that should be capitalized and write the correct capital letter above it.

>   *I*   *N*   *C*   *W*
> **EXAMPLE 1.** I̶ prefer to live in the n̶ortheast, but C̶arlos prefers the W̶est, especially
>   *C*
>   C̶olorado.

1. my dad says that aunt Dorothy was born in Shanghai; that's where she learned to speak chinese.

2. meet us on wednesday, the day after valentine's day.

3. Our team is called the san marcos chargers.

4. We currently live in minnehaha county, but we used to live in turner county.

5. Who can identify the poem that begins, "whenever Richard Cory went downtown"?

6. an acronym for remembering the names of the five great lakes is HOMES.

7. Herman melville once described benjamin franklin thus: "franklin was everything but a poet."

8. dear sir:

9. Jaime moved from Calistoga avenue to fifty-second street.

10. the texas climate is often hot and humid.

EXERCISE B In the following sentences, draw a line through each incorrect capital or lowercase letter and write the correct form above it.

>   *T* *F*   *c*   *c* *P*
> **EXAMPLE 1.** T̶he F̶rench are proud of their C̶apital C̶ity, p̶aris.

1. sincerely yours,

2. I know that janet usually walks her dog, peaches, in the evening.

3. It was in 1830 that Oliver Wendell Holmes, Sr., published the Poem "old ironsides."

4. Do you like you're-the-chef pizza, or should we order a pizza from pizza castle?

5. you are mistaken if you think president Ford was also the President of ford motors.

6. followers of islam read the koran, while jews study the torah.

7. Katrina Gomez, ph.d., is an expert in slavic languages.

8. William Bradford emigrated from england by way of holland aboard the *mayflower*.

9. francis scott key wrote "the star-spangled banner" to commemorate a battle in the war of 1812.

10. my little Brother Javier said that dad gave him permission to eat the whole bowl of salad, but I don't believe him.

Continued ☞

                         Elements of Literature

EXERCISE C   In the following sentences, draw a line through each incorrect capital or lowercase letter and write the correct form above it.

         D   *V*   *S*   *J*   *g*   *s*   *M*

EXAMPLE 1. d̶r. v̶ictor s̶aenz, j̶r., will be our G̶uest S̶peaker next m̶onday.

1. my carrymobile station wagon is nine years old; dad said a newer car would be too expensive.

2. Ali and Bekah are both taking algebra II and latin III this year.

3. If you want to study Art, consider enrolling in the Rhode Island school of Design.

4. ernest hemingway, american author of *the old man and the sea*, lived in ketchum, idaho, among other places.

5. The renaissance was an exciting period in history.

6. The ancient greeks believed in many Gods, including zeus.

7. muslims, not buddhists, celebrate ramadan.

8. the constitution of the united states is a revered historical Document.

9. Surely you jest if you really think that the L.A. lakers are from washington, d.c.!

10. yours truly,

11. Edgar Allan Poe once wrote, "the want of parental affection has been the heaviest of my trials."

12. Henry David Thoreau moved to walden pond in Massachusetts on the fourth of july in 1845; he chose that date deliberately.

13. The first two lines of Robert Frost's poem "nothing gold can stay" are "nature's first green is gold, / her hardest hue to hold."

14. we are going to lost maples state park in october to see the Autumn foliage.

15. dear mr. Rogers:

16. dr. martinez has an advanced degree in Physics, not a Medical degree.

17. The great Poet Robert Frost lived in new England, where he wrote the poem "mending wall."

18. to get to Twenty-Third Street, go south two blocks.

19. Celeste prefers Bakers' Delight Bread, but I prefer to eat bounty of life bread.

20. the reverend penney sutcliff, our new pastor, also happens to be my Aunt.

21. The oregon trail was traveled by our Pioneer forebears, who wanted to settle the west.

22. Ambrose Bierce went South to Mexico to report on the mexican revolution; he was never heard from again.

23. *the new york times* is a well-respected Newspaper.

24. We can't decide whether to attend the special olympics relays or the chili cook-off.

25. The Internal Revenue service and the central Intelligence Agency are two U.S. Government bodies.

LANGUAGE HANDBOOK **12** PUNCTUATION

WORKSHEET 1 | **Using End Marks and Abbreviations (Rules 12 a–e)**

EXERCISE Punctuate abbreviations and supply the correct end marks for the following twenty-five sentences.

EXAMPLES **1.** Are you sure you don't want to do this**?**

2. We live at 105 Lilac St**.**, Grand Rapids, Michigan**.**

1. Ask Mark if he is finished with his online search

2. Do you know Samuel Clemens's pen name

3. I believe it's Mark Twain

4. What a mess you've made

5. Ask Harriet if we should address the envelope to "Dr" or "Mr" Brown

6. The Roman poet and satirist Juvenal was born about A D 60

7. Is Joan of Arc a French national heroine

8. Julius Caesar was assassinated in 44 B C

9. Was the Italian author Giovanni Boccaccio born in 1313 B C or A D 1313

10. Look it up

11. Phooey I was hoping you'd just tell me

12. The American poet E E Cummings is noted for his use of lowercase letters and odd punctuation

13. What are some of his poems

14. Can you tell me who lives at 1600 Pennsylvania Ave, Washington, D C

15. Aunt Matilda rises every day at 5:00 A M

16. The Meadow Run Homeowners' Assn will meet at 7:00 P M

17. Widget, Inc, is the name of Dad's company

18. It is based in Fort Smith, Ark, isn't it

19. Look Dr Dolittle is talking to that armadillo

20. My mom wasn't amused when I added the abbreviation A D to her birthdate on this form

21. Dani lives on Rice St, not Rice Ave

22. Does Mr Sims speak at 11:00 A M or 2:00 P M

23. Is *FBI* the abbreviation for the Federal Bureau of Investigation

24. It has been featured in many television programs

25. Oh This has been way too much fun

LANGUAGE HANDBOOK **12** PUNCTUATION

WORKSHEET 2 | Using Commas (Rules 12 f–l)

EXERCISE A For each of the following sentences, insert commas where they are needed. If a sentence is already correct, write *C* on the line provided.

EXAMPLES _____ 1. Mrs. Castaneda had seen Agnes O'Leary**,** her girlhood friend**,** only a few times since their school days.

_____*C*_____ 2. Their last visit, planned months in advance, had been very enjoyable.

_____ 1. When Agnes appeared unexpectedly at her front door Mrs. Castaneda was delighted to see her again.

_____ 2. She was not so delighted however to see her friend's companion a large shaggy dog that followed at Agnes's heels.

_____ 3. Mrs. Castaneda didn't mind dogs too much but she preferred not to have them in the house.

_____ 4. A retiring quiet person she liked cats much better.

_____ 5. Discovering its image in the hall mirror the dog jumped plunged and barked at its likeness until the women couldn't hear themselves talk.

_____ 6. Mrs. Castaneda wondered why her friend made no move to control her wild pet when it raced around the room scattered the throw rugs and overturned a small table.

_____ 7. When Mrs. Castaneda brought in some cookies the hound leapt at the plate and knocked it out of her hands.

_____ 8. Having greedily devoured the cookies it began to chew the corner of a rug but still Ms. O'Leary did nothing.

_____ 9. Mrs. Castaneda to tell the truth began to wish strongly that her friend and her disorderly animal would take their leave before the house was a total wreck.

_____ 10. Agnes O'Leary it seemed read her thoughts.

_____ 11. Rising from her chair she said, "Well Alicia perhaps we can have a better visit some day when the dog isn't around."

_____ 12. "We're starting back for Elgin Illinois on Saturday March 11 and I may be able to drop in again for a few minutes" she tentatively offered.

_____ 13. Agnes O'Leary put on her coat said goodbye and went out the door.

_____ 14. The dog however had finally curled up in a corner to digest the cookies and Agnes strange to say seemed to be leaving without it.

_____ 15. "Don't forget your dog Aggie," Mrs. Castaneda reminded her friend who was already walking toward her car.

Continued ☞

_____ **16.** The dog had already been there far too long.

_____ **17.** "What do you mean—*my* dog?" Ms. O'Leary exclaimed.

_____ **18.** It turned out that the dog was a stray that had simply wandered in with Ms. O'Leary who had quite naturally assumed that it belonged to the house.

_____ **19.** Mrs. Castaneda who had always been rather timid around dogs shooed the animal from the house with remarkable haste.

_____ **20.** Seven-year-old Juan Castaneda Jr. decided not to ask if he could adopt the stray.

EXERCISE B   In the following sentences, draw a line through any unnecessary commas. If a sentence is already correctly punctuated, write *C*.

EXAMPLES _____ **1.** Judge candidates by their records, not by their speeches, and promises.

_____C_____ **2.** Naturally we should invite Darren, his friend Jerry, and Mona to the party.

_____ **1.** Dr. Alvarez has modern, intelligent, and exciting, ideas about education.

_____ **2.** The things, that we argue about, are, as a matter of fact, quite silly.

_____ **3.** Ms. Levine, our new mayor, is an able, intelligent person, and everyone respects her.

_____ **4.** Try not to yawn, or look at your watch, when you are entertaining guests.

_____ **5.** I am grateful to my violin teacher, of course, who encouraged me to play.

_____ **6.** Facts about philology, linguistics, and semantics, make S. I. Hayakawa's, *Language in Thought and Action*, an informative book.

_____ **7.** Steam is water that has been heated to at least 212 degrees Fahrenheit, and has turned into a gas.

_____ **8.** If you traveled directly south from New Orleans, or Denver, or Los Angeles, you would not touch South America, at any point.

_____ **9.** Amelia Earhart, a famous aviator, left Miami, Florida, on July 1, 1937, in an attempt to fly around the world.

_____ **10.** John Deere, who invented the steel plow, started his business, in Moline, Illinois, which is now the farm-implement capital of the United States.

LANGUAGE HANDBOOK **12** **PUNCTUATION**

| WORSHEET 3 | Using Commas to Separate Items in a Series and with Conjunctions (Rules 12 f–h) |

EXERCISE A   Supply commas where they are needed in the following sentences. If a sentence is already correct, write *C* on the line provided.

EXAMPLES _____ 1. Philippine cuisine is a combination of Malay, Chinese, Spanish, and American dishes.

_____*C*_____ 2. Hiking and swimming are my two favorite activities, but I also enjoy bowling.

_____ 1. Garrett Morgan invented the first traffic signal with red yellow and green lights.

_____ 2. The castles of the Middle Ages were cold damp and dark places.

_____ 3. Devout Jains do not eat meat or fish or eggs.

_____ 4. The only states larger than Montana are Alaska Texas and California.

_____ 5. Mrs. Colombo has a story to prove or disprove almost any political economic or social idea that comes up.

_____ 6. The planes swept over the airport turned gracefully and glided to the runway.

_____ 7. The spoiled child threw himself on the floor and screamed and kicked.

_____ 8. Some Inuit pursue their traditional occupations of hunting fishing and trapping.

_____ 9. Streets were planned homes were built and Brasília was established.

_____ 10. A jury must weigh sift and interpret the testimony of witnesses.

_____ 11. Alligators and crocodiles feed in the water, but they return to land to sun themselves and to breed.

_____ 12. The lighthouse stands on a cold windy lonely part of the island.

_____ 13. Lincoln was born in Kentucky but he spent much of his life in Indiana and Illinois.

_____ 14. Zhang Jie's writing caused controversy enjoyed great popularity and won several awards.

_____ 15. Cocker spaniels are lively friendly intelligent and obedient dogs.

_____ 16. Eric dusted the floors and furniture prepared the meal set the table and waited for his guests.

_____ 17. An energetic little girl was bouncing a large red inflatable ball.

_____ 18. Of all the cities in Puerto Rico, San Juan is the largest Bayamon is second in size and Ponce is third.

_____ 19. The camp is in a beautiful unspoiled region of hills lakes and woods.

_____ 20. Masks are used by African dancers for celebrating harvests acknowledging religious initiations and honoring the dead.

Continued ☞

LANGUAGE HANDBOOK **12** WORKSHEET 3 (continued)

EXERCISE B Insert commas where they are needed in the following sentences. If a sentence requires no additional punctuation, write *C* on the line provided.

EXAMPLE _____ **1.** The Dalai Lama is the religious leader of Tibet**,** but he has been living in exile since 1959.

_____ **1.** The walls were freshly painted and the windows had been washed to finish the redecorating job.

_____ **2.** The two boys became good friends and shared each other's troubles.

_____ **3.** Sap is collected from sugar maples and it is boiled until most of the water has evaporated.

_____ **4.** The Montez family all made tamales for the holidays and they shared them with their friends and neighbors.

_____ **5.** The chipmunk paid no attention to us but continued its morning search for breakfast.

_____ **6.** Mrs. Liu didn't hear me or she didn't care to answer my question.

_____ **7.** One actor forgot his lines yet the performance seemed perfect.

_____ **8.** Uncle Loren eats lots of fruits and vegetables and he exercises every day.

_____ **9.** In the early nineteenth century Anne Royall was America's first crusading journalist who was a woman but she received more scorn than praise for her aggressive reporting.

_____ **10.** The Shawnee chief Tecumseh fought against European settlers moving into the Midwest and he supported the British during the War of 1812.

_____ **11.** We were watching the weather report for we wanted to know the expected path of the hurricane.

_____ **12.** I prepared breakfast for our family and my brother set the table.

_____ **13.** Last night Harvey was repairing the front tire on his bicycle and he discovered several damaged spokes.

_____ **14.** My pen was running out of ink yet I had enough left to finish marking my ballot.

_____ **15.** Was just one person nominated for each class office or were several people nominated for each job?

_____ **16.** Our biology class studied fossils so I tried to find some fossils of my own for my term project.

_____ **17.** Sarah practiced shooting baskets every day, for she planned to try out for the intramural basketball team.

_____ **18.** Donna performed all of the tasks on the checklist and turned on the switch but the lamp still would not work.

_____ **19.** Dad's company has transferred him to Chicago and we will be moving there in a few weeks.

_____ **20.** Albert does not wish to play guitar in the band nor is he interested in being the lead singer.

WORKSHEET 4 Using Commas to Set Off Nonessential Clauses and Participial Phrases (Rule 12 i)

EXERCISE For each item, if the italicized adjective phrase or clause is *essential*, write C. If it is *nonessential*, add commas where they are needed.

EXAMPLES _____ 1. Istanbul**,** *once called Constantinople,* is the largest city in Turkey.

___C___ 2. The nickname *that was associated with Theodore Roosevelt* also became the name of a favorite children's toy.

_____ 1. The Suez Canal *which was completed in 1869* is 107 miles long.

_____ 2. All animals *that have backbones* are classified as vertebrates.

_____ 3. In this city, drivers *who use their horns unnecessarily* are fined.

_____ 4. Saint Nicholas *also known as Santa Claus* is said to bring gifts to children at Chrismastime.

_____ 5. Echo River *which is 360 feet below the surface of the earth* is one of the most fascinating sights of Mammoth Cave.

_____ 6. In our restaurant we serve no food *that we would not eat ourselves.*

_____ 7. Muslims are forbidden to eat anything *containing pork.*

_____ 8. Bristol Park *which is near our home* has a good swimming pool.

_____ 9. Gliders *which are planes without engines* can stay in the air for several hours.

_____ 10. The trucking company will not hire any person *having more than one speeding ticket.*

_____ 11. Students *who plan to attend the job fair* should see Ms. Cohen for further information.

_____ 12. Plymouth Rock *where the Pilgrims landed* is about forty miles from Boston.

_____ 13. Our library weeds out novels *that have not circulated during the past five years.*

_____ 14. Roberto Clemente is credited with over 3,000 hits in his major league baseball career *which spanned eighteen years.*

_____ 15. Emily Dickinson and Robert Frost are two of the poets *that we will study next semester.*

_____ 16. Car crashes *which are much more common than plane crashes* get much less attention in the newspapers.

_____ 17. The presidents *who accomplished most* were severely criticized in their own day.

_____ 18. Caffeine *which is present in both tea and coffee* stimulates the heart and raises blood pressure.

_____ 19. One of the finest civil rights lawyers of his day was Thurgood Marshall *who became the first African American justice on the Supreme Court.*

_____ 20. Marianne Moore was a fan of Muhammad Ali and wrote the jacket liner notes for a record of his *which was released by Columbia Records in 1963.*

LANGUAGE HANDBOOK **12** PUNCTUATION

WORKSHEET 5 Using Commas After Introductory Elements
(Rule 12 j)

EXERCISE A   Supply commas where are they needed after introductory elements in the following sentences.

EXAMPLE **1.** Yes**,** I think we should work today.

1. First let's look at some information about the author.

2. When everyone is settled we'll begin reading.

3. At the beginning of the first paragraph you can find out where James Weldon Johnson was born.

4. Now then who can tell me where he was born?

5. In the upper left-hand corner of page 736 there is a painting of the author.

6. Looking at the details of his face I get the feeling Johnson was a man of quiet determination.

7. Because he was determined to succeed Johnson became the first African American to be admitted to the Florida bar after Reconstruction.

8. Working energetically to promote civil rights Johnson worked as field secretary for the National Association for the Advancement of Colored People (NAACP).

9. During the first phase of the Harlem Renaissance Johnson was an important artistic leader.

10. Well James Weldon Johnson was an interesting man.

EXERCISE B   Insert commas where they are needed in the following sentences. If a sentence requires no additional punctuation, write *C*.

EXAMPLE _____ **1.** After she discovered the comet that is named for her**,** Maria Mitchell became the first woman elected to the American Academy of Arts and Sciences.

_____ **1.** In one Cheyenne myth about how the world was made the coot plays a major role.

_____ **2.** When Dad left for work the house was in perfect order.

_____ **3.** Mules are especially valuable on mountain trails because they are so sure-footed.

_____ **4.** Urged to play by the students Steve sat down at the piano.

_____ **5.** Since a rhetorical question is asked only for effect it doesn't require an answer.

_____ **6.** As Angela opened the door a blast of cold air swept into the room.

_____ **7.** If the United States were to become as densely populated as Great Britain or Japan it would have about two billion people.

_____ **8.** Since some utility companies are given a monopoly in their areas their rates are regulated by the government.

_____ **9.** In most countries of the world you will find the familiar products of American industry.

_____ **10.** Connecting Lake Huron and Lake Superior the Soo is the world's busiest ship channel.

WORKSHEET 6 | **Using Commas (Rules 12 k, l)**

EXERCISE A   Supply commas where they are needed in the following sentences.

> **EXAMPLE 1.** The Alhambra**,** a fortress and palace complex in Spain**,** was built
> in the Middle Ages.

1. La Paz the capital of Bolivia is the world's highest capital.

2. A whale for example is a mammal, not a fish.

3. *Le Jazz Hot* the first magazine devoted entirely to jazz was published in Paris.

4. Please let me know Miss Rowe when you are ready to give your report.

5. Which one are you, John Marks Sr. or John Marks Jr.?

6. Mount St. Helens a volcano in southwestern Washington has erupted several times since 1980.

7. This essay dear reader is not to be taken too seriously.

8. George Eliot's sixth novel *Middlemarch* is of course one of the greatest novels in English literature.

9. Olivia needless to say now wishes that she had studied harder.

10. The Pantheon one of ancient Rome's most famous buildings has been used as a Christian church since the seventh century.

11. The director of the school's computer center does I believe subscribe to both popular and technical computing magazines.

12. Weaver Park long in need of new playground equipment is the focus of the renewal project.

13. Sherlock Holmes and John H. Watson M.D. live at 221 B Baker Street London England.

14. It is very doubtful however whether Leo a quiet person will speak.

15. Pocahontas the daughter of Powhatan married John Rolfe instead of John Smith.

16. By the way Sylvia be sure to let me know if you can go.

17. The Liberty Bell cracked when it was tolled for the funeral of Chief Justice John Marshall who died July 6 1835 in Philadelphia.

18. Ms. Knox the elementary school principal pointed out that the students after all were children not mature adults.

19. On August 13 1818 Lucy Stone pioneer of American women's rights was born in West Brookfield, Massachusetts.

20. Dear Vita

    Did you read the story that I sent you?

    Your friend

    Virginia

Continued ☞

LANGUAGE HANDBOOK **12** **WORSHEET 6** *(continued)*

EXERCISE B   Provide commas where they are needed in the following sentences.

EXAMPLE 1. Mr. Conrad Wills, Sr., will visit Enterprises, Inc.

1. Dear Mom

2. On Sunday November 2 we will have our annual get-together.

3. Pat Sparks RN moved here from Scottsdale Arizona.

4. Address the letter to 2604 Sycamore Lane Duluth MN 55811.

5. With love

Debra

6. Juanita Flores M.D. is a surgeon.

7. Our business will move to 142 W. 52nd St. New York New York at the end of the month.

8. My dad was born in Parker South Dakota in 1950.

9. Mark Jefferson Jr. is my brother.

10. On Saturday July 4 1998 my little sister hit her first home run.

11. Was February 29 1996 an important day in history?

12. Matthew and Darla would like you to be on their team Sally.

13. Watch for the grand opening of SuperClothes Inc. in a mall near you!

14. Tomorrow, we will invite the neighbors the ones who just moved here to go with us.

15. Dear Aunt Louisa and Uncle Angelo

16. Carlos has a straight-A average in American history; nevertheless he is studying hard for the test on Friday.

17. Joe be sure your income tax return is postmarked by 12:00 midnight on April 15.

18. Our dog Tuxedo likes to visit our veterinarian Dr. Roger Walker Jr.

19. Please mail this package to WaterSave Ltd. 317 Tacoma St. Tulsa OK 74127.

20. Kathy would you take these books over to New Books, Old Books Etc. for me?

21. Dashiell Hammett who lived from 1894 to 1961 was an American writer.

22. We left Detroit Michigan on the six o'clock flight for Atlanta Georgia.

23. Have you ever seen the aspens around Cloudcroft New Mexico change color in the fall?

24. These tickets are for 8:30 P.M. January 5 instead of 8:30 A.M. January 6.

25. My uncle Roy Hall Sr. goes by the nickname "Pop."

LANGUAGE HANDBOOK **12** **PUNCTUATION**

WORSHEET 7 | Using Semicolons (Rules 12 m–p)

EXERCISE A   Insert semicolons where they are needed in the following sentences.

> **EXAMPLES 1.** The pre-Civil War period and the postwar period fell between 1850 and 1900; many of the events of that era had a profound effect on our country.
>
> **2.** Several interesting and important happenings took place between 1850 and 1900; for example, there were literary, cultural, and historical events.

1. Manufacturing helped the United States become a world leader in business in addition, business and agriculture grew as the population moved west.

2. Novels published during that era include *Uncle Tom's Cabin*, by Harriet Beecher Stowe *The Adventures of Huckleberry Finn*, by Mark Twain and *The Red Badge of Courage*, by Stephen Crane.

3. *The Adventures of Huckleberry Finn*, Mark Twain's sequel to *The Adventures of Tom Sawyer*, further developed the character of Huck Finn and Huck, as well as the novel itself, has since become an American literary staple.

4. Sojourner Truth was an abolitionist and women's rights advocate she dictated *Narrative of Sojourner Truth* around 1850.

5. Other influential women of the era were Susan B. Anthony and Elizabeth Cady Stanton, who became coleaders of the U.S. women's rights movement Clara Barton, who organized the American Red Cross and Harriet Beecher Stowe, who published *Uncle Tom's Cabin*, an influential novel about slavery.

6. Alexander Graham Bell patented the first telephone in 1876 Thomas Edison invented the first phonograph in 1877.

7. In 1863, President Abraham Lincoln delivered his short but forceful speech, the Gettysburg Address, at the dedication of a Civil War cemetery and by April 1865, Lincoln was dead, assassinated in Ford's Theater, Washington, D.C.

8. Over in India, the British continued to rule the subcontinent as a result, a large-scale uprising against British rule, called the Sepoy Rebellion, occurred in the 1850s.

9. In England, Charles Darwin published *Origin of Species* in 1859 in it, Darwin explained his groundbreaking theory of evolution.

10. France's Gustave Flaubert published *Madame Bovary* in 1856 this classic realistic novel caused quite a sensation because of the moral issues it raised.

Continued ☞

LANGUAGE HANDBOOK 12 WORKSHEET 7 (continued)

EXERCISE B In the following sentences, insert semicolons where they are needed.

> **EXAMPLE 1.** Lillian Hellman was considered one of the finest dramatists of her time**;** her plays include *Watch on the Rhine*.

1. We rehearsed every afternoon every day our confidence increased.

2. Veena started for the telephone suddenly, she changed her mind.

3. I must get eight hours' sleep I feel miserable the next day otherwise.

4. Raisins are dried grapes prunes are dried plums.

5. We work hard on our lawn unfortunately, the results are very discouraging.

6. Hebrew reads from right to left Chinese reads from top to bottom.

7. Hay made from pasture grass is lower in protein than hay made from alfalfa and clover as a result, cows may be given a variety of feed.

8. The wise are so uncertain the ignorant are so positive.

9. A blanket produces no heat it merely retains the heat of the body.

10. Education must include the whole person otherwise, it is not true education.

11. Dad was issued a new computer at work the mouse, however, won't be delivered until sometime next week.

12. We had hoped, by the way, to leave on time we have plans for the evening.

13. John Updike's successful novels include the following books in his Rabbit series: *Rabbit, Run,* 1960 *Rabbit Redux,* 1971 *Rabbit is Rich,* 1981 and *Rabbit at Rest,* 1990.

14. Later, the detective found the old files and began reviewing the evidence he felt that something had not been checked out thoroughly.

15. The farmer herded the sheep into the next field he left the cattle where they were.

16. On our vacation we drove to Washington, D.C. we stopped along the way to see the Liberty Bell in Philadelphia, Pennsylvania, and the museums in Baltimore, Maryland.

17. Jasmine and Li are practicing their roles for tomorrow's mock debate if you are interested, they will be the first pair to argue their case.

18. For the next two weeks, I will be working on my math fair project I have been able to keep my topic a secret so far.

19. Three great Russian writers whose works appeared during the last half of the nineteenth century are Leo Tolstoy, author of *War and Peace* Fyodor Dostoyevsky, author of *The Brothers Karamazov* and Anton Chekhov, author of *The Sea Gull*.

20. The golf tournament was interrupted by a weather delay thunderstorms moved into the area.

LANGUAGE HANDBOOK **12** **PUNCTUATION**

| **WORKSHEET 8** | Using Commas and Semicolons (Rules 12 h, m) |

EXERCISE   In the following sentences, change commas to semicolons wherever two sentences are run together without a conjunction to connect them, and add commas wherever they have been omitted from compound sentences containing conjunctions. If a sentence is already correct, write *C* on the line provided. Do not change or add any words.

EXAMPLES   ___*C*___   **1.** The Krolskis liked mushrooms but found them too expensive to serve very often.

_____   **2.** One day Mrs. Krolski was struck by a bright idea; she stopped at the library and checked out books on the identification of mushrooms.

_____   **3.** She studied the books night after night, and she learned which fungi are edible and which are not.

_____   **1.** The following Sunday the Krolskis went to a nearby forest, after a long search they found a large number of mushrooms among some decaying logs.

_____   **2.** Mrs. Krolski applied every test she had learned and found many mushrooms of the same, edible type.

_____   **3.** The baskets were soon full and the family started for home.

_____   **4.** Her husband peered in her basket, he asked if the mushrooms were safe to eat.

_____   **5.** Eva said they were fine, they were the variety *Fistulina hepatica* shown in her book.

_____   **6.** Her husband's question had taken away her appetite for mushrooms so she decided not to serve them for supper that night.

_____   **7.** As the Krolskis were eating breakfast the next morning, the mail carrier arrived.

_____   **8.** "Why not give some mushrooms to Mr. Mullins?" suggested Mrs. Krolski. "We're eating downtown tonight and they may not last until tomorrow."

_____   **9.** Mr. Mullins thanked the Krolskis profusely and walked away with his gift.

_____   **10.** The next morning the mail carrier came, but it wasn't Mr. Mullins.

_____   **11.** Mr. Krolski wondered where Mr. Mullins was, he feared the worst.

_____   **12.** The man said that Mr. Mullins had called in sick, the Krolskis' hearts sank.

_____   **13.** Mr. Mullins had several young children and they could have eaten mushrooms, too.

_____   **14.** Mr. Krolski felt very guilty, a cold sweat broke out all over him.

_____   **15.** Mrs. Krolski went to her office but couldn't keep her mind on her work.

_____   **16.** She imagined that she heard the agonizing groans of the man she had sickened.

_____   **17.** As the Krolskis were trying to eat their breakfast the next morning, they suddenly heard the familiar voice of Mr. Mullins.

_____   **18.** "Good morning," he said. "I wrenched my back as I was changing a tire yesterday morning but I feel much better today."

_____   **19.** "Good!" exclaimed the Krolskis with unusual feeling, they really meant it.

_____   **20.** The Krolskis had no more appetite for mushrooms and they never ate them again.

LANGUAGE HANDBOOK 12 PUNCTUATION

WORKSHEET 9 Using Semicolons and Colons (Rules 12 m–r)

EXERCISE A Supply semicolons and colons where they are needed in the following items.

> **EXAMPLE 1.** Please arrive no later than 5:30; the bus will leave shortly thereafter.

1. The magazine article "Colds How to Avoid Them" looks like something you might want to read.

2. Dear Sir or Madam

3. My report on F. Scott Fitzgerald is done however, I still need to proofread it one more time.

4. The capital cities of Europe that we will be visiting are listed on the itinerary London, England Paris, France and Rome, Italy.

5. During the nineteenth century, an era of great social change, many great writers added their voices to the American scene but the ones I love most, Emily Dickinson and Walt Whitman, were pioneers of unconventional verse forms.

EXERCISE B Supply semicolons and colons where they are needed in the following sentences.

> **EXAMPLES 1.** Let's discuss Frederick Douglass first; afterward, we can talk about Harriet Tubman.
>
> **2.** *Harriet Tubman: Conductor on the Underground Railroad* is a biography for young readers.

1. In *My Bondage and My Freedom*, Douglass writes about songs of slavery later on, these songs were referred to as "sorrow songs" by writer W.E.B. DuBois.

2. Spirituals deal with issues of freedom they address spiritual freedom as well as physical freedom.

3. Here are some examples of well-known spirituals "Go Down, Moses" and "Follow the Drinking Gourd."

4. Hector titled his essay on spirituals "Songs of Slaves Our Cultural Heritage."

5. He hopes to hand in his report before the late bell rings at 8 40.

6. Hector begins his essay in the form of a letter whose first sentence is as follows "Let my people go."

7. Hector's essay captures the imagination of his class his teacher gives him the highest grade.

8. Many people were referred to as Moses during the time of slavery for example, in her work with the Underground Railroad, Harriet Tubman's code name was Moses.

9. Exodus 2 1–10 tells about the baby Moses being hidden in the bulrushes he was rescued by the daughter of the pharaoh.

10. Other essays students turned in were "Sojourner Truth Voice of Freedom," by Denice Jones "All Points North," by Albert Jefferson and "Long Road to Freedom," by Kevin Sullivan.

| WORSHEET 10 | Test (Rules 12 a–r) |

EXERCISE A   Punctuate the following items correctly, including end punctuation.

EXAMPLE 1. Hey! Don't forget to call Barry, Dexter, and Rhonda.

1. Quick Light the fire sweep the floor and do the dishes

2. Please call me before 10 A M

3. Are you sure you don't care for any more broccoli

4. Let's ask Dad if we can have the car tonight Mom doesn't need it

5. Your loving son

6. Frannie do you know Isabella's new address

7. Please have your work done Joel by 5 30

8. Is Chris Bradley Sr a relative of yours

9. No I don't think so however I have many distant cousins I've never met

10. Yours truly

11. On Thursday November 26 1998 my sister Jeanie made her noisy entrance into the world

12. In his teens and twenties the writer Jack London had many adventures

13. Today Jack London is known for his exciting fast-paced adventure stories

14. I have read London's novel *White Fang* and I will read his short story "To Build a Fire" tomorrow

15. *The Call of the Wild* my favorite Jack London novel is a well-written tale of survival

16. My youngest brother who is an avid reader also loves this novel

17. While reading London's story about the Yukon I got chilly so I put on a sweater

18. They live at 2132 Loma Vista St Kansas City Missouri however I'm not sure what the ZIP Code is

19. Do you know what important event an event at school happened to me last week

20. Sharon's instructions were forceful "Get up now!"

21. You forgot these items your book your homework and your thinking cap

22. Do you know Felicia what time it is

23. No I don't because my watch doesn't work it needs a new battery

24. Here are the poems you will read for homework "Design," by Robert Frost "Shine, Perishing Republic," by Robinson Jeffers and "Bells for John Whiteside's Daughter," by John Crowe Ransom

25. In his essay on realism Gary Q. Arpin makes an observation about the scant output of literature on the Civil War "Very little important poetry and fiction issued directly from the Civil War, largely because few major American writers experienced the war firsthand. . . . The 'real war' would not find a place in American fiction until the development of the realistic novel."

Continued ☞

EXERCISE B   Punctuate the following items correctly, including end punctuation.

EXAMPLE 1. Tell me, Henry, what is today's date?

1. Should we address you as Dr Natasha Jones

2. Harold Brown Jr always writes his year of birth thus A D 1984

3. Dear Susie

4. Sit down Leilani and make yourself comfortable

5. Wow Look at her go

6. Well Morgan I don't know where Selena is I haven't seen her since 1 30 P M

7. Dear Mr Lee

      I am writing to inquire about the summer job opening at your company.

8. Your little sister is a curious endearing child however she talks too much

9. My grandparents who lived in a small town all their lives traveled extensively

10. I like to eat Thai food and I also like Italian-style dishes such as pasta primavera

11. My dogs' names are Fifi Fluffy and Fido

12. Please write to me at 13701 Spartan Way Austin TX 78746

13. I met my best friend Pat Tuesday September 1 1998 on the first day of school

14. I read an informative article called "Armadillos Those Highway Heroes"

15. My dad works for Medics Inc which is in Tulsa

16. Thinking about all the things I enjoy doing I sometimes have a hard time deciding what to do

17. By the end of this week I hope to be caught up with all my work

18. My poem "About Leaves" is about not surprisingly leaves

19. Having talked to you I feel much better now

20. Mrs Burton I need some extra time to finish my poem my muse is on vacation

21. Yes I suppose you may have two extra days

22. For our review let's list books and their authors *Moby-Dick*, by Herman Melville *The Scarlet Letter*, by Nathaniel Hawthorne and *Walden or Life in the Woods*, by Henry David Thoreau

23. During the course of this unit we have read the work of many writers such as Emerson Thoreau and Hawthorne but one writer Herman Melville especially stands out for me

24. Mrs Burton's voice could be heard down the hall "Everyone needs to hand in an original poem by Tuesday."

25. The author indicates that not every American writer received acclaim during his or her life "Kate Chopin's work went unrecognized, and was even scorned, during her lifetime. Along with many other literary pioneers, Chopin never lived to see her work vindicated."

WORKSHEET 1 | Using Italics (Rules 13 a, b)

EXERCISE   In the following sentences, underline the titles, words, characters, letters, numbers, and symbols that should be italicized.

> **EXAMPLES 1.** Remember, <u>i</u> before <u>e</u> except after <u>c</u> or when sounded like <u>a</u> as in <u>neighbor</u> and <u>weigh</u>.
>
> **2.** My favorite movie is <u>Lawrence of Arabia</u>.

1. Juanita can explain the difference between to and too.

2. Woman Making Tortillas was painted in 1945 by Mexican artist Diego Rivera.

3. Our theater group is putting on a production of Thornton Wilder's Our Town.

4. Steven Spielberg's movie Schindler's List is a powerful portrayal of the Holocaust.

5. Because of its political emphasis, the comic strip Doonesbury is put on the editorial page in some newspapers.

6. Is this supposed to be a lowercase l, a capital I, or the number 1?

7. The motto on the United Kingdom's royal arms, Dieu et mon droit, is French for "God and my right."

8. I use Microsoft® Word on my computer for word processing.

9. Homonyms are words that sound alike, such as rain, rein, and reign.

10. We plan to travel on the Orient Express, a train with a rich history.

11. The court is reviewing the Garcia v. Pope case.

12. Spirit of St. Louis is not a ghost that haunts St. Louis, but rather a famous airplane.

13. The USS Constitution was a battleship memorialized by Oliver Wendell Holmes in a poem.

14. The Jazz Singer, one of the first sound films with dialogue, opened in 1927.

15. Rodgers and Hammerstein's groundbreaking musical play Oklahoma! opened in 1943.

16. The British warship Guerrière was involved in the War of 1812.

17. Galileo is the name of a spacecraft, as well as the name of a great scientist.

18. The Octopus, by Frank Norris, is a novel about wheat farmers fighting the railroad.

19. T. S. Eliot edited a literary magazine called The Criterion.

20. We read the Odyssey last year, but I have yet to read Homer's other epic poem, the Iliad.

21. We are watching a dramatization of Joseph Conrad's novel Nostromo on Masterpiece Theatre this evening.

22. Check out the story in our free weekly paper, The Austin Chronicle.

23. I have an old copy of Aerosmith's Toys in the Attic album.

24. Don't confuse sole with soul.

25. Mozart wrote his Symphony No. 1 in 1765 when he was only nine years old.

LANGUAGE HANDBOOK	**13** **PUNCTUATION**

WORKSHEET 2 | **Punctuating Quotations (Rule 13 c)**

EXERCISE   On the line provided, punctuate and capitalize each *direct* quotation. For *indirect* quotations, add correct end punctuation and write *I* on the line provided.

EXAMPLES **1.** Was it Eleanor Roosevelt who wrote you must do the thing you think you cannot do *Was it Eleanor Roosevelt who wrote,* **"**You must do the thing you think you cannot do**"?**

2. Mr. Park believes that the third most widely used language in the United States is American Sign Language**.** *I*

1. These brakes are unsafe warned Mr. Pesina _____

_____

_____

2. Mr. Pesina warned us that our brakes were unsafe _____

_____

_____

3. How can I improve my grade Pam asked her teacher _____

_____

_____

4. Pam asked her teacher how she could improve her grade _____

_____

_____

5. Pam asked her teacher how can I improve my grade _____

_____

_____

6. I always enjoy speaking to students began the speaker _____

_____

_____

7. The driver explained that his radio wasn't working _____

_____

_____

8. Don't invest on the basis of tips or rumors advised the stockbroker _____

_____

_____

Continued ☞

9. When shall I meet you Fred asked _____
_____

10. Ruben asked when did the architect I. M. Pei immigrate to the United States _____
_____
_____

11. Selfishness is the greatest curse of the human race said William Gladstone _____
_____
_____

12. Mrs. Boltz asked Aaron and me if we would like to go sailing _____
_____
_____

13. Would you mind giving me this recipe Wesley asked after he tasted the gazpacho _____
_____
_____

14. What beautiful craftsmanship exclaimed Ms. Kudelski when she saw the Olmec ceramics ____
_____
_____

15. Was it P. T. Barnum who said that there's a sucker born every minute _____
_____
_____

16. I think it was Michelangelo who said that trifles make perfection, and perfection is no trifle __
_____
_____

17. How exciting Yolanda exclaimed when she heard she had been accepted at the Summer Arts
Institute _____
_____

18. When Dane answers the phone, he asks are you there _____
_____
_____

19. Can't you just hear Mr. Leone saying he told us so _____
_____
_____

20. I've always been shy of singing confessed Mabel Mercer _____
_____
_____

LANGUAGE HANDBOOK **13** PUNCTUATION

WORKSHEET 3 Punctuating Quotations (Rule 13 c)

EXERCISE In the following sentences, correct errors in capitalization and punctuation: commas, quotation marks, periods, question marks, and exclamation points.

EXAMPLE 1. "Did you have fun," Darryl asked, "on your camping trip?"

1. Janine said Yes, it was great! My aunt's family lives in Virginia, so we met at Shenandoah National Park for a family reunion

2. Janine continued We hiked, biked, and swam; and, taking turns, we cooked our meals on a camp stove. I always think food tastes best when it's cooked outdoors

3. Did you Raquel asked see any snakes

4. No Janine admitted we didn't see any snakes, but there was a bear

5. Darryl exclaimed A bear I can't believe you saw a bear

6. Well Janine said let me tell you the whole story. There had been a few bear sightings, so the park rangers suggested we stow all of our food and sleep with clean pots and spoons in our tents

7. Why Tanika asked would you need pots and spoons in your tent

8. To use as noisemakers if any bears wandered into our campsite Janine explained

9. My cousin she continued woke me in the middle of the night and asked did you hear that? I did hear something tromping through the leaves. It sounded like a very big bear, and it sounded very close to our tent

10. What did you do Darryl asked

11. We beat on the pots and yelled of course replied Janine but it kept coming

12. Did your parents wake up asked Raquel. Did your dad scare the bear away

13. Yes and no. He couldn't understand why we were making such a racket, so he came to our tent Janine continued

14. Oh no Darryl groaned did he run right into the bear

15. No Janine replied he came to our tent and saw us huddled together squealing and beating on those pots. He just started to laugh

16. He laughed Raquel queried. What did he find so funny

17. He wondered answered Janine why we were trying to scare away the deer

18. A deer Tanika exclaimed

19. Yes said Janine a deer. Actually there were several deer eating leaves from the trees behind our tent. Because of all the dry leaves on the ground, the deer had made as much noise as a bear

20. Darryl laughed I think your adventure illustrates the power of suggestion

LANGUAGE HANDBOOK 13 PUNCTUATION

WORSHEET 4 Punctuating Titles (Rules 13 a, b, d)

EXERCISE In the following sentences, punctuate the titles correctly by using underlining for italics or by using quotation marks.

EXAMPLES 1. Have you read the biography <u>The Life of Emily Dickinson</u>?
2. My favorite short story is "Guests of the Nation" by Frank O'Connor.

1. Sunrise, Sunset is a popular song to play at weddings.

2. William Faulkner wrote the short story A Rose for Emily.

3. Tragically, the U.S. space shuttle Challenger exploded soon after liftoff in 1986.

4. For an informative article on weed control, read Weeds Be Gone.

5. Langston Hughes published his first poetry collection, The Weary Blues, in 1926.

6. Did you see the episode No Way Out on TV last night?

7. For tomorrow, we have to read portions of Ralph Waldo Emerson's essay Self-Reliance.

8. I read an article in Fitness magazine called Walk Yourself to Health.

9. We sang Happy Birthday at Paula's party.

10. Ars poetica is a Latin term meaning "the art of poetry."

11. Ars Poetica is also the title of a poem by Archibald MacLeish.

12. T. S. Eliot's influential long poem The Waste Land was published in 1922.

13. I wonder who will be on the cover of Time magazine this week?

14. Rip Van Winkle is a well-known story by Washington Irving.

15. I titled my essay A Slice of Life.

16. We are reading in our book the section titled The American Renaissance.

17. Every Sunday evening, we watch 60 Minutes.

18. I'm on the chapter titled And So Forth.

19. Aberdeen American News is a small-town newspaper with features on local events.

20. Amazing Grace is often sung a cappella, which means without instrumental accompaniment.

21. The symbol & is called an ampersand and is often used in place of the word and.

22. Many consider Arthur Miller's play Death of a Salesman to be his best work.

23. When I was a child, The Wizard of Oz was my favorite movie.

24. Many office workers enjoy the comic strip Dilbert because it pokes fun at corporate culture.

25. Open your books to the chapter titled Adjectives and Adverbs.

LANGUAGE HANDBOOK 13 PUNCTUATION

WORKSHEET 5 Using Apostrophes to Show Possession (Rule 13 f)

EXERCISE A For each of the following word groups, add an apostrophe where it is needed.

EXAMPLES ___*father's*___ **1.** my fathers book

___*girls'*___ **2.** those girls bicycles

___*children's*___ **3.** a childrens party

_____ **1.** a womans voice

_____ **2.** the womens voices

_____ **3.** a childs interests

_____ **4.** the Feldmans dog

_____ **5.** one cashiers mistake

_____ **6.** both parents consent

_____ **7.** a rabbis menorah

_____ **8.** most mens coats

_____ **9.** two weeks pay

_____ **10.** Herman Melvilles novel

_____ **11.** a schools reputation

_____ **12.** both drivers brakes

_____ **13.** George Washington Carvers research

_____ **14.** these babies parents

_____ **15.** your moneys worth

_____ **16.** a childrens game

_____ **17.** the boys locker room

_____ **18.** Jorges *charro* suit

_____ **19.** the peoples choice

_____ **20.** Saudi Arabias oil reserves

_____ **21.** those girls friends

_____ **22.** those employees pensions

_____ **23.** the mans hobby

_____ **24.** both referees decisions

_____ **25.** nobodys fault

EXERCISE B Add apostrophes where they are needed to show the possessive in the following sentences.

EXAMPLE **1.** It is anyone's guess whose gloves those are.

1. Just put in five dollars worth of gas for now.

2. If this is nobodys hat, then we can give it to someone who needs it.

3. That is my mother-in-laws music box on the dresser.

4. Thoreaus and Emersons writings are American classics.

5. Kayla has done about an hours worth of work on the project so far.

6. That is Uri and Sashas lively new puppy.

7. I think it is somebody elses turn to read.

8. Toms and her car is the bright red one.

9. Dunn, Waller, and Jones advertising firm is doing quite well this year.

10. Grandma and Grandpas motorcycle is parked out front.

Elements of Literature

LANGUAGE HANDBOOK **13** **PUNCTUATION**

WORSHEET 6 | **Using Apostrophes to Form Contractions (Rule 13 g)**

EXERCISE A Form contractions from the following word groups by inserting apostrophes where they are needed. Write your answers on the lines provided.

EXAMPLE _*they've*_ **1.** they have

_____ **1.** we will

_____ **2.** how is

_____ **3.** there is

_____ **4.** Sean is

_____ **5.** 1999

_____ **6.** will not

_____ **7.** he is

_____ **8.** he has

_____ **9.** are not

_____ **10.** could have

_____ **11.** she is

_____ **12.** we have

_____ **13.** they are

_____ **14.** I am

_____ **15.** would not

_____ **16.** you are

_____ **17.** it is

_____ **18.** I will

_____ **19.** is not

_____ **20.** they will

EXERCISE B In the following sentences, underline the correct word or contraction in parentheses.

EXAMPLES **1.** (*They're*, _*Their*_) lights are off, so I assume (_*they're*_, *their*) not home tonight.

2. If the club (_*lets*_, *let's*) us work on the float, (*lets*, _*let's*_) work as hard as we can.

1. (*They're, Their*) going to Bombay for (*they're, their*) son's wedding.

2. (*You're, Your*) face gets red when (*you're, your*) angry.

3. (*It's, Its*) tail will wag when (*it's, its*) happy.

4. (*Who's, Whose*) the lucky person (*who's, whose*) column was chosen?

5. (*Let's, Lets*) flip a coin to see who (*let's, lets*) in the cat.

6. (*They're, Their*) working hard on (*they're, their*) garden.

7. (*It's, Its*) a badly trained dog that won't come when (*it's, its*) master calls.

8. (*You're, Your*) happiest of all in (*you're, your*) own home.

9. (*Who's, Whose*) the girl (*who's, whose*) talking to Mr. Muñoz?

10. (*It's, Its*) nice to know that Kathy trained her puppy away from (*it's, its*) habit of chewing visitors' shoelaces.

WORKSHEET 7   Using Apostrophes (Rules 13 f–h)

EXERCISE A   For each of the following sentences, correctly write on the line provided each word that requires an apostrophe. If a sentence is already correct, write *C*.

EXAMPLE _____*shareholders'*_____ **1.** Those shareholders concerns were addressed at the meeting.

_____ **1.** The coyote was licking its pups.

_____ **2.** The way she pronounces her *a*s tells me shes from Boston.

_____ **3.** Teresa often makes 7s that look like 2s.

_____ **4.** One of Mexicos best known authors of fiction is Carlos Fuentes.

_____ **5.** The mens and womens locker rooms are downstairs.

EXERCISE B   For each of the following sentences, correctly write on the line provided each word that requires an apostrophe.

EXAMPLE _*I'm, people's, aren't*_ **1.** After working in the lost-and-found department, Im astonished at peoples carelessness with their belongings as well as at their honesty in returning things that arent theirs.

_____ **1.** When articles are found around the school, theyre brought to our office.

_____ **2.** If—after thirty days wait—the article isnt claimed, the finder may keep it as his or hers.

_____ **3.** We search the contents of every article to find the name of its owner, but often theres no identification to be found.

_____ **4.** Sometimes there are initials on jewelry, but there could be fifty J. J.s in our school.

_____ **5.** We cant help wondering what could have been in students minds when they brought to school and lost such unusual articles as a violin case full of jigsaw puzzle pieces.

_____ **6.** What must the teachers assignment have been to bring forth such peculiar articles?

_____ **7.** It stimulates ones imagination!

_____ **8.** At the end of the year when the schools office is about to close, many dollars worth of unclaimed clothing is turned over to the Helping Hand Society.

_____ **9.** Weve often wondered how its possible for a person to lose a perfectly good overcoat without even noticing its loss or bothering to inquire for it.

_____ **10.** Its a mystery, too, why a student buys an expensive new pen yet makes no effort to recover it when its lifes work has barely started.

Elements of Literature

LANGUAGE HANDBOOK	13 PUNCTUATION

WORKSHEET 8 Using Hyphens, Dashes, Parentheses, and Brackets (Rules 13 i–n)

EXERCISE A Use hyphens to show where the following words can be divided. If a word cannot be divided, write *ND* on the line provided.

EXAMPLE _twen-ty_ **1.** twenty

_____ **1.** conquered   _____ **11.** malleable

_____ **2.** ballad   _____ **12.** scientific

_____ **3.** alone   _____ **13.** evade

_____ **4.** future   _____ **14.** contribution

_____ **5.** dreamed   _____ **15.** vicinity

_____ **6.** forty-five   _____ **16.** zoological

_____ **7.** generally   _____ **17.** progressive

_____ **8.** ignore   _____ **18.** clumped

_____ **9.** staffed   _____ **19.** bulletproof

_____ **10.** lighten   _____ **20.** seventy-six

EXERCISE B Supply hyphens, dashes, parentheses, and brackets where they are needed in the following sentences.

EXAMPLES **1.** I believe that sixty ‿ five votes ‿ out of eighty ‿ six votes cast ‿ makes for a three ‿ fourths majority.

2. Samuel Clemens ‿ also known as Mark Twain ‿ 1835–1910 ‿‿ wrote *The Adventures of Huckleberry Finn*.

1. Jacques is twenty one years old.

2. Many of my favorite foods spinach pizza, enchiladas, and Greek salads are on the menu.

3. James Thurber 1894–1961 is regarded by some people as the foremost American humorist of the twentieth century.

4. It looks as though a two thirds majority has prevailed.

5. Edward Estlin E. E. Cummings was born in Cambridge, Massachusetts.

6. Many of the people in our group of friends Paula, Jorge, Saul, and Nick are learning Russian.

7. Willa Cather 1873–1947 wrote about immigrant families on the Midwestern prairie.

8. The good condition of this bike it ought to bring at least a few dollars at the garage sale should make it easy to sell.

9. All of my siblings Steve, Tom, Katy, Kevin, and Jean keep in touch with each other.

10. Elizabeth Bishop was born in 1911. See photo on page 1034.

13 PUNCTUATION

WORKSHEET 9 | Test (Rules 13 a–n)

EXERCISE A   Supply all the missing punctuation marks in the following sentences. *Note:* Do not use semicolons.

> EXAMPLE **1.** While they were on their way to the grocery store, Mrs. Spencer turned to her daughter Clarice and said**,** **"**Let**'**s stop at the bank to deposit my paycheck.**"**

1. As Mrs. Spencer entered the bank, she noticed that it looked peculiarly quiet and deserted there wasnt a teller, officer, or customer to be seen anywhere.

2. After about fifteen minutes another customer a man in a hurry entered the bank.

3. He looked about him in a puzzled way and asked Wheres everybody today

4. It does seem strange, sir said Mrs. Spencer that no ones around. Ive already been waiting over fifteen minutes.

5. Maybe the banks been held up he exclaimed The employees may be locked up in the vault.

6. Feeling very frightened, Mrs. Spencer grabbed her childs hand and rushed to the telephone that was on the managers desk.

7. Soon the police arrived their guns were drawn and plunged through the doors of the bank.

8. After an exhaustive search of the bank, the police captain said This is Veterans Day, and all the banks are closed. Apparently, the guard forgot to lock up last night.

9. The captain phoned Mrs. Bailey she's the manager and told her that she should come to the bank and lock up.

10. A bank the captain said is a bad place to leave unlocked with no one around.

EXERCISE B   Punctuate the following sentences correctly.

> EXAMPLES **1.** Mrs. Baxter said**,** **"**Have you read <u>The Optimist's Daughter</u>, a novel by Eudora Welty?**"**
>
> **2.** Sandra**'**s favorite movie ‾_∧ the one she**'**s seen eight times ‾_∧ is <u>Titanic</u>.

1. Its easy to confuse accept and except, because theres not much difference in pronunciation.

2. To toast someones health, some people use the French expression à votre santé.

3. Artist Andrew Wyeth painted Quaker Ladies.

4. William Carlos Williams 1883–1963 wrote the poem The Red Wheelbarrow.

5. My stepfathers age is thirty eight.

6. It was two years ago today I mean three that we first met.

7. Your hs look like ns when you write hastily.

8. I am three fourths of the way through Herman Melvilles novel Moby-Dick.

Continued ☞

9. Bernard Malamuds story The Magic Barrel is about a Jewish rabbinical student, Leo Finkle.

10. Shoe is Kevins favorite comic strip.

11. The French word fils pronounced feece means "son" and is used after proper names to distinguish a son from his father of the same name.

12. Everybodys glad thrilled is more like it that youre coming to visit us.

13. Jackson wants to install the software program CorelDRAW!™ on his computer.

14. Its not easy to read your capital Is.

15. My three favorite writers John Steinbeck, Albert Camus, and Jane Austen are all novelists.

16. Read the chapter Our American Heritage for tomorrows discussion.

17. In a famous speech Patrick Henry said, I know not what course others his fellow patriots may take; but as for me, give me liberty, or give me death!

18. Toby named his small airplane The Plain Plane.

19. Ask Harry I mean Larry if anyones seen Mary.

20. Theyd counted eighty eight egrets by noon.

21. Nevermore is the refrain in Poes poem The Raven.

22. Cant you sing Twinkle Twinkle Little Star just one more time?

23. John Adamss dying words were Thomas Jefferson still survives.

24. Your half page report which is rather short is somewhat lacking in development.

25. Howards copy of the novel The Great Gatsby is dogeared.

EXERCISE C   Punctuate the following sentences correctly.

> EXAMPLE 1. Twenty ˰seven ˰ make that twenty ˰eight ˰ people are in this room.

1. Both Terrys and Lees 7s sometimes look like ls.

2. Everyones going to the rock opera Tommy.

3. There are thirty two students in Shawnas class.

4. My little brother that boy over there in the red shirt just turned ten.

5. Carl Sandburg 1878–1967 is the author of the popular poem Chicago.

6. Four score and seven that's 87 years ago are the opening words to a famous speech of Abraham Lincolns.

7. Ill invite my cousins that would be Tess, Caroline, and Donnie to our party.

8. Were learning to play the traditional song Greensleeves on the guitar.

9. My father-in-laws favorite vacation was on the Orient Express, which once ran from Paris to Istanbul.

10. Ive borrowed Kims edition of the epic poem the Aeneid.

LANGUAGE HANDBOOK **14** **SPELLING**

| WORSHEET 1 | **Using Word Parts (Rules 14 a–c)**

EXERCISE Divide each of the following words into parts (prefixes, roots, and suffixes). Then, write a definition based on the meanings of the parts. A dictionary may be used to find the meanings of word parts.

EXAMPLE **1.** bioplasm _bio | plasm—living matter_ _____

1. emit _____

2. interview _____

3. amoral _____

4. diagnosis _____

5. counselor _____

6. biotechnology _____

7. ruination _____

8. islander _____

9. mismanage _____

10. exportation _____

11. conducting _____

12. remitter _____

13. transportation _____

14. interstate _____

15. atypical _____

16. editor _____

17. induct _____

18. misinformation _____

19. correctable _____

20. intertribal _____

21. philosophy _____

22. thermometer _____

23. protoplasm _____

24. coauthor _____

25. antihero _____

Elements of Literature

NAME _____ CLASS _____ DATE _____

LANGUAGE HANDBOOK **14** SPELLING

| WORSHEET 2 | Using Spelling Rules (Rules 14 d–f)

EXERCISE A Fill in the blanks with the correct letters: *ie, ei, cede, ceed,* or *sede.*

EXAMPLE **1.** v____*ei*____n

1. pat_____nt
2. w_____ght
3. ex_____
4. p_____rced
5. retr_____ver
6. super_____
7. defic_____ncy
8. rec_____ved
9. pre_____
10. _____ghteen

11. dec_____ve
12. ch_____ftain
13. s_____zure
14. perc_____ve
15. v_____l
16. pro_____ing
17. v_____w
18. n_____ghborly
19. bel_____vable
20. for_____gn

EXERCISE B For each of the following sentences, write the misspelled word correctly on the line provided. If a sentence is already correct, write *C.*

EXAMPLE _*efficiently*_ **1.** My new sewing machine stitches efficeintly.

_____ **1.** Niether of the boys worked on the science project last weekend.

_____ **2.** People who live in northern climates long ago learned to survive in feircely cold winters.

_____ **3.** A new line of passenger planes is expected to superceed current models.

_____ **4.** Be sure to save your sales reciepts in case you want to return any items.

_____ **5.** Empathy usually will succeed in settling disputes between friends and family members.

_____ **6.** "Have you really seen the cieling in the Sistine Chapel?" Harriet asked in awe.

_____ **7.** You can depend on music's being a major part of our nieghborhood picnics.

_____ **8.** Darla and Kyle said that thier grandfather was once a guide at the Grand Canyon.

_____ **9.** Numerous earth tremors had been reported in the region, so scientists brought in a seismograph.

_____ **10.** Mr. Evans finally conseded that my geometric proofs were at least partially correct.

LANGUAGE HANDBOOK 14 SPELLING

WORKSHEET 3 | Adding Prefixes and Suffixes (Rules 14 g–m)

EXERCISE A On the line provided, spell each of the following words with the given prefix or suffix.

EXAMPLE **1.** wire + ing = _____*wiring*_____

1. recur + ed = _____   **11.** rob + er = _____

2. lease + able = _____   **12.** farce + ical = _____

3. simplify + ed = _____   **13.** toy + ing = _____

4. picnic + ing = _____   **14.** inter + urban = _____

5. tie + ing = _____   **15.** day + ly = _____

6. puffy + ness = _____   **16.** outrage + ous = _____

7. un + necessary = _____   **17.** il + legible = _____

8. sly + ly = _____   **18.** dye + ing = _____

9. fancy + ful = _____   **19.** awe + ful = _____

10. mis + state = _____   **20.** snippy + ly = _____

EXERCISE B For each of the following sentences, write the misspelled word correctly on the line provided. If a sentence is already correct, write *C*.

EXAMPLE *prohibited* **1.** Sharon was prohibitted from attending the club meetings until she paid her dues.

_____ **1.** Gabriel's pig may win first place because it is definitely the bigest in the livestock show.

_____ **2.** What was the total mileage of your trip from New Hampshire to Georgia?

_____ **3.** Listening to Jeremy's commencement speech was a deeply moveing experience for everyone in attendance.

_____ **4.** "Our arguement was silly and childish, and I apologize," Shawn said.

_____ **5.** The missing package was not traceable because it was not insured or registered.

_____ **6.** Tonya paniced when she saw the shadows on the kitchen wall.

_____ **7.** James Baldwin decryed how the world often undervalues a writer's talents.

_____ **8.** A good director can help actors and actresses learn the perfect timeing of their lines.

_____ **9.** The frogs in the pond normaly don't croak loudly during cold evenings.

_____ **10.** Norman is happyest when he is playing his drums.

LANGUAGE
HANDBOOK **14** SPELLING

WORKSHEET 4 | **Forming Plurals of Nouns (Rule 14 n)**

EXERCISE A On the line provided, spell the plural form of each of the following nouns.

EXAMPLE **1.** glass _____*glasses*_____

1. navy _____
2. proof _____
3. Chinese _____
4. seven-year-old _____
5. veto _____
6. Franz _____
7. apartment _____
8. 1800 _____
9. Cassidy _____
10. junkyard _____

11. igloo _____
12. child _____
13. donkey _____
14. day lily _____
15. copy _____
16. butterfly _____
17. alga _____
18. calf _____
19. soprano _____
20. scratch _____

EXERCISE B For each of the following sentences, write the misspelled word correctly on the line provided. If a sentence is already correct, write *C*.

EXAMPLE _*aircraft*_ **1.** Few large aircrafts fly into the old airport these days.

_____ **1.** Both architects design houses with patioes for outdoor dining.

_____ **2.** The truck was running out of gas, and all the service stations were closed.

_____ **3.** I wonder how many states have more than two hundred countys.

_____ **4.** Did all the classes see the film about the importance of corn to settlers in North America?

_____ **5.** This salad tastes particularly good because of the fresh tomatos and mushrooms.

_____ **6.** The gooses flew over the area and circled twice before landing in one of the open fields.

_____ **7.** My ancestors emigrated from Ireland and Norway in the late 1700s.

_____ **8.** The Gradyes admire the work of Mexican artist Diego Rivera.

_____ **9.** Glenda gave me two booksmark that state "So many books, so little time."

_____ **10.** If you want to participate in formal debates, you should learn how to state hypothesises clearly.

LANGUAGE HANDBOOK **14** **SPELLING**

WORKSHEET 5 **Forming Plurals of Nouns (Rule 14 n)**

EXERCISE A   On the line provided, spell the plural form of each of the following nouns or words used as words.

EXAMPLE **1.** McJoy _____ *McJoys* _____

1. turnkey _____

2. loaf _____

3. chairman _____

4. Mason jar _____

5. fish _____

6. Marks _____

7. headdress _____

8. solo _____

9. radio _____

10. lass _____

11. bounty _____

12. *or* _____

13. potato _____

14. Plains Indian _____

15. 1760 _____

16. fife _____

17. brother-in-law _____

18. lash _____

19. ellipsis _____

20. toolbox _____

EXERCISE B   For each of the following sentences, write the misspelled word correctly on the line provided. If a sentence is already correct, write *C*.

EXAMPLE _____ *Mounties* _____ **1.** Members of the Royal Canadian Mounted Police are known as Mountys.

_____ **1.** "Yes, horseflys are troublesome to horses," the vet said.

_____ **2.** The painting depicts the Siouxes moving their camps across the plains.

_____ **3.** Why do historians use the adjective *roaring* to describe the 1920s?

_____ **4.** His collection included several pearl-handled knifes and a sword from the Civil War.

_____ **5.** "How many Romeoes does one Juliet usually encounter?" the professor asked.

_____ **6.** The astronomer said that many celestial phenomenon involve planetary objects.

_____ **7.** Even the runners-up in the contest receive substantial prizes, including a trip to Hawaii.

_____ **8.** It's my understanding that four tardys equal one absence, but I could be wrong.

_____ **9.** My grandfather has notchs on his favorite belt for each of his three grandchildren.

_____ **10.** When the curtain went up, the stage was bare except for two pianoes and a sitar from India.

Elements of Literature

LANGUAGE HANDBOOK **14** SPELLING

| WORKSHEET 6 | Test (Rules 14 a–n)

EXERCISE A   Proofread the following sentences, and circle any misspelled words. On the line provided, write the misspelled words correctly. If a sentence does not contain any spelling errors, write *C*.

  EXAMPLE 1. Surely you will (conceed) that the play was (aweful)! *concede, awful*

1. We should look closely at our heros and think about what has driven them to sucede. _____
_____

2. "For the second year in a row, the Mayers held a lovly Christmas party," Charlene sayed. _____
_____

3. The mosquitoes multiplied rapidly because there were many water-filled containers in the yard.
_____

4. All of the five-years-old looked up hopefuly at the teacher, who was understanding but firm. __
_____

5. It was certainly surpriseing to find only mice and donkies in the horse barn. _____
_____

6. The Andersons want to take a liesurely vacation in the Bahamas next year. _____
_____

7. Casa Jimenez, a favorite restaurant in my nieghborhood, serves wonderful nachoes. _____
_____

8. Cary must overcome her shyness if she wants to succeed at the cheerleading tryouts. _____
_____

9. The weather conditions are advantagous for the crew to set sail. _____
_____

10. The Juarezs readyly agreed to chaperone the party in the school cafeteria Friday night. _____
_____

EXERCISE B   Proofread the following sentences, and circle any misspelled words. On the lines provided, write the misspelled words correctly. If a sentence does not contain any spelling errors, write *C*.

  EXAMPLE 1. I have a great (admireation) for Navajo arts and crafts. *admiration*

1. Both traditional and new arts and crafts of the Navajo are especially beautyful. _____
_____

2. Navajo womens weave absolutely gorgeous blankets and rugs. _____
_____

Continued ☞

3. I'm sure you would consede that their styles are quite varyed. _____

_____

4. According to a fascinateing legend, Spider Woman taught them to weave using natural elements.

_____

5. These elements included sun rays and lightning. _____

_____

6. Familys that own Navajo weavings are realy lucky. _____

_____

7. Some Navajo jewelry, too, has been highly prized for many years. _____

_____

8. The bold designs and large pieces of precious stone in the jewelry are unmistakeable. _____

_____

9. Some people might think that Navajo bracelets wiegh too much to be worn comfortably. ____

_____

10. Navajo sand paintings glued on boards also have recieved much interest in recent years. ____

_____

EXERCISE C   Proofread the following sentences, and circle any misspelled words. On the lines provided, write any misspelled words correctly. If a sentence does not contain any spelling errors, write *C*.

EXAMPLES   ___*mice, busily*___   **1.** The (mouses) are (busyly) building their nests this time of year.

___*C*___   **2.** We harvested the green tomatoes last night because the temperature was forecast to drop below freezing.

_____   **1.** On their trip to New Mexico, the Smiths noted the milage between each pueblo they visited.

_____   **2.** I occasionally use chopsticks at Chinese restaurants, but I forget to practice at home.

_____   **3.** The governor encourages communication and openess within all of the state's countys.

_____   **4.** Hikeing to the naturally heated pools became a dayly ritual for the couple.

_____   **5.** The hardware store carries several different lengths of tape measures, but I quickly found the one I wanted.

Continued ☞

_____ **6.** Our lilac bushs are in full bloom this year and are lovly.

_____ **7.** Apparently a jam occured when too many trayes were placed on the conveyor belt at lunch.

_____ **8.** The apartment complexs are side by side, but they have different owners.

_____ **9.** "You have exceded your privileges because your hall passes are used up," Mrs. Shannon said.

_____ **10.** The mooses stared at us for a few minutes and then disappeared behind the leafs of the trees.

EXERCISE D Most of the following sentences contain misspelled words. On the lines provided, write any misspelled words correctly. If a sentence does not contain any spelling errors, write *C*.

EXAMPLES _____*awfully*_____ **1.** The chances are awefully good that you have a favorite Dr. Seuss book.

_____*C*_____ **2.** Many of us are now reading Dr. Seuss's books aloud to our younger brothers and sisters and to the children we baby-sit.

_____ **1.** All ages, from threes-year-old to senior citizens, enjoy the deceptivly simple stories of Dr. Seuss.

_____ **2.** It's fairly safe to procede with that assumption, I believe.

_____ **3.** After all, the universality of Dr. Seuss is among the least challengeing hypothesis.

_____ **4.** His zany storys are admired worldwide by readers, from the Japaneses to the Americans.

_____ **5.** Have you heard the joiful news that the public now have a new Dr. Seuss book, years after the author's death?

_____ **6.** It may sound wierd, but then childrens and adults expect that from Dr. Seuss!

_____ **7.** Dr. Seuss left sketchs and some verse on his bulletin board.

_____ **8.** Dr. Seuss's books are respectted by other writers.

_____ **9.** My favorite Seuss book is titled *Green Eggs and Ham*.

_____ **10.** I'm sure his latest book, about a school where students learn how to think, won't linger on bookshelfs.

WORKSHEET 1 | **Common Usage Problems**

EXERCISE A   Underline the word or expression in parentheses that is correct according to standard, formal usage.

> **EXAMPLE** **1.** Neither the lioness (*or*, *nor*) her cubs seemed to notice the camera crew.

1. Karen had never given a speech before, but she did extremely (*well*, *good*).

2. I wish you (*could of*, *could have*) seen how fast the flamenco dancer clicked her castanets.

3. (*Regardless*, *Irregardless*) of the citizens' wishes, the city intends to put a street through the meadow.

4. The newspaper article questions (*whether*, *if*) the troubled amusement park will reopen.

5. The boss wondered what (*affect*, *effect*) the computer problems would have on productivity.

6. "(*Everyone*, *Every one*) knows our distinguished speaker, Coretta Scott King," the president said.

7. The librarian was pleased by the large (*amount*, *number*) of books that had been checked out.

8. With lighting and quick hand motions, the magician created many (*allusions*, *illusions*) that thrilled the audience.

9. Darren's great-grandparents (*emigrated*, *immigrated*) from Poland in the late 1800s.

10. The couple decided that the bright red trim looks (*bad*, *badly*) with the light blue house siding.

EXERCISE B   Most of the following sentences contain at least one error in usage. For each sentence, draw a line through the error(s) and then write the correct word(s) on the line provided. If a sentence is already correct, write *C*.

> **EXAMPLE** _____*Almost*_____ **1.** ~~Most~~ everyone agreed that the music was too loud.

_____ **1.** The plant food should be stirred in a half a gallon of water.

_____ **2.** You can bring this here newspaper with you when you leave.

_____ **3.** It's likely that the meeting will be canceled because of the snow.

_____ **4.** Each and every one of the intricately carved totem poles was more than ten feet tall.

_____ **5.** "Do you intend to lay on the couch the rest of the day?" Mother asked.

_____ **6.** I don't think that Leah meant to infer that you're sweater looks old.

_____ **7.** In my opinion, those kind of joke just isn't funny, Milton.

_____ **8.** It will take a while to walk to the ruins because the distance is further than the guide said.

_____ **9.** Matamoros it is a city in Mexico across the Rio Grande from Brownsville, Texas.

_____ **10.** The coach contrasted the different batting styles of the two veteran players.

LANGUAGE HANDBOOK **15** **GLOSSARY OF USAGE**

| WORKSHEET 2 | **Common Usage Problems**

EXERCISE A   Underline the words or expressions in parentheses that are correct according to standard, formal usage.

> **EXAMPLE 1.** What (*type*, *type of*) salad dressing do you usually use?

1. The whole family is going to the reunion in Florida (*accept, except*) me.

2. I've (*all ready, already*) decided (*who's, whose*) my favorite in the talent show.

3. Mr. Blevins worked overtime and is therefore (*some, somewhat*) exhausted.

4. Do you know the difference (*among, between*) a cheetah, a cougar, and a panther?

5. Mr. Gray (*taught, learned*) the class about wampum, beads used as money by North American Indians.

6. I don't want to go bowling; (*beside, besides*), I have to work late tonight.

7. "I don't feel (*good, well*), so I'm going to rest today," Liam said.

8. Surprisingly, the students talked (*like, as if*) they had never heard of the Supremes.

9. The carpenters (*rose, raised*) the wooden beams over (*there, their*) heads.

10. "Now that we are (*all together, altogether*)," the instructor said, "let's begin the lesson."

EXERCISE B   Most of the following sentences contain at least one error in usage. For each sentence, draw a line through the error(s) and then write the correct word(s) on the line provided. If a sentence is already correct, write *C*.

> **EXAMPLE** _____*since*_____ **1.** You can leave early ~~being as~~ you've finished your homework.

_____ 1. We can go to the beach and/or the park tomorrow.

_____ 2. Please give me the broken bowl that fell off the dining room table.

_____ 3. Joseph Bruchac he writes a lot about American Indian cultures.

_____ 4. Ben observes the speed limits like he was instructed to do.

_____ 5. You can sit the boxes of books on the floor and go onto the next project.

_____ 6. I read where Mark Twain's real name was Samuel Clemens.

_____ 7. Yes, there's an Indian restaurant in town, but it's a long way from here.

_____ 8. "I can't help but think that too much television is harmful to children," the senator said.

_____ 9. Our German shepherd is larger then the greyhound next door.

_____ 10. Where was the injured manatee at when the divers rescued it?

WORKSHEET 3   Test

EXERCISE A   Underline the words or expressions in parentheses that are correct according to standard, formal usage.

> EXAMPLE **1.** Stephen Crane's novel *The Red Badge of Courage* had a powerful (*affect, effect*) on me.

1. (*Besides, Beside*) Alana, I was the only one in the class who had ever gone on a whale watch before today.

2. The scientists said that on the next program they will have (*farther, further*) discussion about the nature of time and space.

3. It seems foolish to me, but Julio intends to hike the trail around the lake (*irregardless, regardless*) of the rain.

4. (*Who's, Whose*) names are actually on the contract and the loan for the new house?

5. Jerry Lee thinks that (*either, any one*) of the three race cars will go faster than his dad's car.

6. The rabbi met with the caterers to make sure that the food for the banquet is (*all together, altogether*) kosher.

7. "We are expecting a large (*number, amount*) of copper wiring to be delivered this afternoon," the store manager said.

8. Some mornings I (*lie, lay*) in bed for as long as thirty minutes after the alarm goes off, and then I have to hurry to get ready for school.

9. (*A lot, Much*) of the artwork in the new museum exhibit about life in the inner city is by young African American artists.

10. Dave said that he would (*learn, teach*) me the difference between an alligator and a crocodile.

EXERCISE B   Most of the following sentences contain errors in usage. For each sentence, draw a line through the error(s) and then write the correct word(s) on the line provided. If a sentence is already correct, write *C*.

> EXAMPLE _____*would have*_____ **1.** Sheila ~~would of~~ gone swimming with the others, but she had to work.

_____ **1.** Wayne admitted that he is kind of anxious about the results from the achievements tests, but I'm sure he did good.

_____ **2.** Yes, you are correct that the Hawaiian word *aloha* is used as a greeting and/or a farewell.

_____ **3.** The washing machine motor sounds like it is spinning out its very last load.

_____ **4.** Mr. Larsen inferred that Megan had received assistance on her homework, but he didn't actually say so.

Continued ☞

_____ 5. Do you know if the labels on all of the canned goods are printed in both Spanish and English?

_____ 6. If you ask me, neither Marvin or Tisa will be chosen to represent the club in the pancake-eating contest anyways.

_____ 7. "You may think that the vinegar smells badly, but it is an excellent cleaning agent," Mom said.

_____ 8. The announcement specifically states that anyone may attend the open house and that a purchase isn't required.

_____ 9. You're right that in colloquial language "a jam" is a difficult situation.

_____ 10. Carla is the server which we nominated for the award due to her efficiency.

EXERCISE C   Underline the words or expressions in parentheses that are correct according to standard, formal usage.

EXAMPLES   1. "Please (*bring, take*) these tapes to the library when you return your books," Erica said.

2. "If you're going to be here for dinner, please stop at the supermarket and (*bring, take*) home a gallon of skim milk," said Mother.

1. In social studies, we read (*where, that*) the American Civil War was fought from 1861 to 1865.

2. (*This, This here*) magazine article states that a new fad among students is the wearing of African medallions.

3. Do you prefer the (*type, type of*) laundry detergent that is perfumed or unperfumed?

4. Many people with determination have (*risen, raised*) above the disadvantages of their circumstances.

5. Since I changed piano teachers, my playing has improved (*some, somewhat*), but it would be even better if I practiced more.

6. "I have waited (*a half, half*) an hour for service in a restaurant, but never a full hour!" Charlotte said.

7. We frequently ate plantains after returning from Puerto Rico, but we don't have them much (*any more, anymore*).

8. (*Being as, Because*) you enjoy political discussions, I thought you would like to come to the rally with us this evening.

9. (*Most, Almost*) all of the rocks were knocked off the wall when the five frightened deer tried to clear the top.

10. The fog swirling around the base of the trees played tricks on our vision and created an eerie (*allusion, illusion*).

Continued ☞

LANGUAGE HANDBOOK 15 WORSHEET 3 (*continued*)

EXERCISE D   Most of the following sentences contain errors in usage. For each sentence, draw a line through the error(s) and then write the correct word(s) on the line provided. If a sentence is already correct, write *C*.

EXAMPLE   ___*Those*___   1. ~~Them~~ crows are squawking and walking all over the yard, and they are quite comical.

_____   1. Try and understand that only one person can get the job, even if each and every one of the applicants is qualified.

_____   2. Rex, my new puppy, has a rather bewildered expression, but he is probably much smarter then he looks.

_____   3. "If you would just sit the dishes on the counter after drying them, I will put them away," Mrs. Davidson said.

_____   4. In my paper, I plan to compare the poetic style of Rita Dove to that of Maya Angelou, discussing their similarities and differences.

_____   5. Whitney and I had walked all the farther we could, but we still had a long ways to go.

_____   6. To our amazement, the agile youth jumped off of the trampoline and somersaulted on to the floor in only a few seconds.

_____   7. Hao, my best friend, hopes that her parents will be able to immigrate from Cambodia this year.

_____   8. While theirs is probably the more popular song of the two, I can't help liking yours better.

_____   9. Like people say, practice really does make perfect.

_____   10. I gladly except your offer to go to the party because there should be some great music their.

_____   11. Max he was already to leave for school and wondered where the bus was at.

_____   12. You had ought to be on time for work irregardless of the heavy traffic.

_____   13. Zina and Paolo can teach you and you're friends how to bowl after school each and every day this week.

_____   14. Mom must of left the porch light on because she knew we would be sort of late getting home.

_____   15. Did Leah and Roberto collect less newspapers than every one else?

_____   16. You can tell by there symbols that these kind of plastic can be recycled.

_____   17. See if you can get farther along with your group work today than you did yesterday.

_____   18. Barbara she tried to judge how her choice between an apple, a pear, and an orange might effect her appetite.

_____   19. Jared could of given anyone of us a ride home if we had of waited for him.

_____   20. How many guests will be setting in the audience when we walk on to the stage?

DATE DUE
